CREATIVE STRATEGIES IN
FILM SCORING

Ben Newhouse

Berklee
Press

FILM CREDITS

Cops (1922)
Presented by Joseph M. Schenck
Written and Directed by Buster Keaton and Eddie Cline

Pacific Crest Trail Documentary
Hiker: Owen Rojek
Narrator: Ben Newhouse
Photography and Videos by Owen Rojek, Opera George, and Travis Roe

All music composed and produced by Ben Newhouse.

BERKLEE PRESS

Editor in Chief: Jonathan Feist
Senior Vice President of Online Learning and Continuing Education/CEO of Berklee Online: Debbie Cavalier
Vice President of Enrollment Marketing and Management: Mike King
Vice President of Academic Strategy: Carin Nuernberg
Editorial Assistant: Emily Jones

ISBN 978-1-5400-0073-6

Study music online at
online.berklee.edu

DISTRIBUTED BY

HAL•LEONARD®
7777 W. BLUEMOUND RD. P.O. BOX 13819
MILWAUKEE, WISCONSIN 53213
Visit Hal Leonard Online
www.halleonard.com

1140 Boylston Street
Boston, MA 02215-3693 USA
(617) 747-2146

Visit Berklee Press Online at
www.berkleepress.com

CONTENTS

ACKNOWLEDGMENTS

Special thanks to: Debbie Cavalier, Carin Nuernberg, Boriana Alexiev, Steve Harding, Mike King, Jonathan Feist, Jessie Cappuccilli, Dan McFadden, John Scotti, Craig Reed, Jeri Sykes, Matthew Nicholl, Alison Plante, Sean McMahon, Francisco Noya, Robert Lau, Fred Sturm, Mike Post, Alan Ett, Scott Liggett, Ryan Neill, Tim Aarons, Irl Sanders, Levon Broussalian, Doug Wood, Owen Rojek, Phil Sheeran, Rachel Albert, Allison Thomas, my beautiful wife Katie, and our bundle of energy Bryce.

PREFACE

When I first began teaching film scoring, I encountered students asking probing questions about the creative process. "How did you come up with that idea?" Or... "How can I consistently come up with good ideas for any kind of scene?" It became clear to me that students needed a systematic method to guide the creative process, most significantly when their teacher was no longer around to provide guidance.

Truth be told, most creative decisions in film scoring are made through some combination of instinct, trial and error, and experience. Unfortunately, each of these methods has drawbacks and limitations. Instinct is problematic in collaborative environments, where the instincts of one professional may not align with those of others working on the project. Trial and error is slow and inconsistent. Experience is wonderful, but it takes years to develop. Experience can also create friction in collaborative environments where experience levels differ, and the inexperienced may not wish to automatically defer to the experienced. When attempting to answer my students inquiries about the creative process, the combination of instinct, trial and error, and experience felt like an insufficient answer. Subsequently, my goal became to develop a systemic process for making creative decisions in film scoring. This book is the eventual outcome of that pursuit.

Once the goal became to formalize the creative process, I found inspiration in an unlikely place: corporate strategy. At one point along my personal journey, I completed a masters in business administration. During this study, I noted an unexpected similarity between film score professionals and corporate strategists. Both professionals work on a project to project basis. In both cases, a given project may have very little in common with the professional's previous projects. The critical success factors for any project may be wholly different from any project the professional had previously encountered.

I also noted that the corporate strategist has tools the composer did not—a set of frameworks used to analyze companies and industries. Each framework is a series of questions designed to reveal important information about a business or an industry. The frameworks are general enough to apply to any business, but specific enough to provide the analyst with actionable information. So the corporate strategist does not rely solely on instinct, trial and error, and experience. Rather, the strategist can proceed systematically through the frameworks to observe key information about the project and develop ideas.

This book endeavors to offer such a tool to students and creative professionals in film scoring. The book details a framework for making creative decisions, so the creative team need not "start from scratch" on every project. Notably, the framework is not intended for film composers alone. Rather, the framework can be used by anyone faced with the question, "What should the music for this film be?" My sincere hope is that the framework helps many creative professionals conceive the perfect music for their projects.

FILMS REFERENCED IN THIS BOOK

Throughout the book, a wide variety of films are mentioned as references. In each case, the musical score demonstrates a key concept discussed in the text. In addition to providing a relevant example, they are all entertaining and engaging films. Copyright restrictions unfortunately prohibit our inclusions of this music. However, if you wish to view them, they are listed here, in the order in which they are discussed:

- *Slumdog Millionaire* (Fox Searchlight, 2008)
- *Crouching Tiger, Hidden Dragon* (Sony Classics, 2000)
- *Avatar* (Twentieth Century Fox, 2009)
- *Atlantis: The Lost Empire* (Walt Disney Feature Animation, 2001)
- *Fight Club* (Twentieth Century Fox, 1999)
- *Brokeback Mountain* (Focus Features, 2005)
- *Back to the Future* (Universal Studios, 1985)
- *Sense and Sensibility* (Columbia Pictures, 1995)
- *The Matrix* (Warner Brothers, 1999)
- *Troy* (Warner Brothers, 2004)
- *Raiders of the Lost Ark* (Paramount, 1981)
- *Alien* (Twentieth Century Fox, 1979)
- *Aliens* (Twentieth Century Fox, 1986)
- *Snow White and the Seven Dwarfs* (Walt Disney Productions, 1937)
- *Beauty and the Beast* (Walt Disney Feature Animation, 1991)
- *Frozen* (Walt Disney Animation Studios, 2013)
- *Shrek* (DreamWorks, 2001)
- *Superbad* (Columbia Pictures, 2007)
- *The Green Mile* (Warner Brothers, 1999)
- *Braveheart* (Paramount, 1995)
- *Jaws* (Universal Pictures, 1975)
- *The Lion King* (Walt Disney Feature Animation, 1994)
- *Heat* (Warner Brothers, 1995)
- *Monsters, Inc.* (Pixar Animation, 2001)

- *Star Wars Episode III: Revenge of the Sith* (Twentieth Century Fox, 2005)
- *Jurassic Park* (Universal Studios, 1993)
- *Sinbad: Legend of the Seven Seas* (DreamWorks, 2003)
- *Saving Private Ryan* (DreamWorks, 1998)
- *Inception* (Warner Brothers, 2010)
- *The Truman Show* (Paramount Pictures, 1998)
- *Antz* (DreamWorks, 1998)
- *Air Force One* (Columbia Pictures, 1997)
- *Charade* (Universal Pictures, 1963)
- *Pulp Fiction* (Miramax, 1994)
- *Hook* (TriStar Pictures, 1991)
- *Schindler's List* (Universal Pictures, 1993)
- *My Girl* (Columbia Pictures, 1991)
- *Apollo 13* (Universal Pictures, 1993)
- *Cops* (1922)
- *Planet Earth* (British Broadcasting Corporation, 2006)
- *The National Parks: America's Best Idea* (Public Broadcasting Service, 2009)

ABOUT THE MEDIA FILES

To access the accompanying audio, video, and blank worksheet files that accompany this text, go to www.halleonard.com/mylibrary and enter the code found on the first page of this book. This will grant you instant access to every example. Examples with accompanying media are marked with the following icons:

Audio

Video

CHAPTER 1

Framework

The goal of this book is to introduce and detail a decision-making framework for film scoring. The framework is six factors to be considered before selecting or composing a piece of music for film. After progressing through the framework in a thoughtful manner, the creative team will have identified the most vital characteristics of the music they wish to create.

Framework Steps

The six steps to the framework are:

1. Style
2. Emotion
3. Energy Level
4. Dialogue/Sound Effects
5. Contour
6. Form

Style is the overall genre of the music, such as rock, hip-hop, Celtic, or orchestral film music.

Emotion answers the question "What do we want the audience to feel?" Notably, emotion and style are often muddled together in casual conversation. For instance, the term "love theme" may be cited as a musical style. However, it is best to separate the two concepts. A love scene could be scored with orchestral music, rock, or another musical style. Likewise, orchestral film music can be triumphant, sad, adventurous, terrifying, or another emotion. Musical style and emotional genre are two fundamentally different concepts and should be treated separately in the decision-making process.

Energy level identifies how much activity is in the visuals and determines how the music should enhance that activity.

Dialogue and *sound effects* are the other audio elements in the film. The creative team must decide how to structure the music so that it complements the other audio elements.

Contour is how changes in the music are synchronized with changes in the picture. For instance, aligning a musical hit with a picture cut is a contour decision.

Form is how all the music in a film is organized. For instance, using the same melody in all scenes involving a certain character is a form decision.

The framework can be used in two different contexts. First, composers can use the framework to guide their creative process. The framework adds structure to creative decision-making, enabling composers to get an effective result consistently and quickly. Second, the framework can be used to guide deliberations within a creative team. Often, a communication barrier exists between musicians and non-musicians working in film. Musicians think in terms of musical language—melody, rhythm, harmony, counterpoint, and orchestration. Meanwhile, non-musicians think in terms of story, plot, acting—and may not be able or inclined to discuss advanced musical composition techniques in specific detail. To bridge this divide, each step of the framework is a general artistic concept equally palatable to musician and non-musician, allowing all team members to express their creative opinion. Yet despite being general artistic concepts, the framework leads a trained composer to a specific set of musical ideas.

After testing the framework across thousands of professional and academic projects, I can happily report that it yields effective results. Composers who use the framework develop a specific idea about what music is needed for a scene. Creative teams who use the framework are able to minimize differences and build consensus.

In this book, we will dedicate a full chapter to each step of the framework. Last, we will conduct two case studies that apply the framework to specific scenes. We will view each scene without music, consider each step of the framework, and then view the scene with music created based on the framework analysis.

CHAPTER 2

The Creative Team

Films are made by large groups of people. Rather than individual self-expression, films are the result of collective group expression. Likewise, the precise nature of any piece of music in a film is the result of the opinion and input of multiple creative professionals. In this chapter, we will detail the creative professionals typically involved in the creation of a film score. Notably, no two creative teams are alike. Exactly who makes a given musical decision depends on the personalities, experience levels, and personal practice of all team members.

PRODUCER

A film producer is someone who oversees the creation of a film, providing high-level supervision during all stages of production. Producers take on a wide variety of roles, including raising funds, securing the cinematic rights to a book or story concept, overseeing script development, and hiring key creative personnel. Producers have the authority to make creative decisions as they deem appropriate. A producer may have an opinion about what composer to hire, what musical style to employ, or what popular songs to incorporate into a soundtrack.

DIRECTOR

A director manages the day-to-day creation of the film, focusing on the creative aspects of the filmmaking process. The director is heavily involved in all stages of the production process and is tasked with organizing all creative team members around a single vision. The director works closely with the composer and other members of the musical team, offering feedback, advice, and suggestions. While directors do not typically compose music, their input and advice strongly influences the direction of a score.

FILM EDITOR

The film editor is tasked with selecting shots and assembling the full-length film. Traditionally, the film editor is not considered a member of the music team. However, it can occur that a film editor adds music to a film while editing. Though such music is intended to be temporary, ideas from temporary music often influence other decision-makers and work their way into the final film. A director may hear temporary music, develop a taste for a particular idea, and then instruct the composer to create something similar. In such a scenario, the film editor impacts the creative direction of the music more than their job description implies.

MUSIC SUPERVISOR

A music supervisor selects music for use in a film. Music supervisors are most heavily involved in films that use songs and other preexisting music. Typically, music supervisors scour the catalogues of record labels and music libraries looking for just the right track for a scene. After finding the appropriate track, music supervisors arrange the necessary contracts and legal permissions to use the music.

COMPOSER

A composer composes new music for a film. Despite writing the actual music, the composer rarely exerts total creative control over a score or even an individual cue. All decisions by the composer are made in close consultation with the director and other creative team members. Often, it is the composer's role to assess the collective opinion of the creative team and write music that realizes the team's vision. In the case of competing visions, the composer can facilitate decision making by writing multiple pieces of music, allowing the creative team to assess more than one potential final product. The collaborative environment of film scoring differs from the oft-romanticized image of a composer— a creative genius working in isolation who emerges from a dark room with a finished masterpiece. Composers working in film must set aside this romanticized view and embrace the collaborative nature of film scoring.

ORCHESTRATOR

An orchestrator works on a composer's team. Orchestrators take a sketch created by the composer, which may be a MIDI computer file or a condensed notated score, and generate the fully notated score that supports a recording session. Ultimately, it is up to each composer/orchestrator team to determine how to divide up tasks, and an orchestrator can impact creative decisions when the composer allocates significant tasks to the orchestrator.

MUSIC EDITOR

A music editor is given a wide variety of tasks that impact creative decisions. Traditionally, the music editor assembles a temp score in close consultation with the director. Temp scores help the creative team solidify creative direction and provide a seemingly finished film for test screenings. Music editors also edit any preexisting music so that it conforms to the picture. When changes are requested after music has been recorded, the music editor will edit the recorded music to accommodate these requests.

ASSISTANTS

All of the professionals above may have assistants. The exact duties of an assistant depend on the personal practices of the supervising professional. The assistant may be tasked with fetching coffee, updating computer software, or helping compose a piece of music. Nonetheless, assistants frequently contribute at least marginally to the decision-making process in film.

SUBJECTIVITY, OBJECTIVITY, AND DISCUSSION

Complicating the creative team's task is a simple reality—film scoring is an inherently subjective art form. For any individual scene, there is more than one effective solution. If you give a scene and identical instructions to two professional composers, the resulting scores would not be identical pieces of music. However, they would likely share some fundamental musical characteristics, and it is plausible that both scores would be effective musical solutions for the scene. As such, there is more than one "right answer" for any scene.

Of course, there are also choices that can objectively be deemed ineffective. One can imagine scoring a medieval drama with contemporary jazz or a serious love scene with upbeat circus music. These choices would universally be deemed inappropriate. So, while there are multiple effective solutions, there are also objectively ineffective solutions. As a mental construct, the creative team can imagine that they have a limited set of right answers from which to choose and a separate set of ineffective answers that they should avoid.

It is the goal of the framework to guide decision-makers to the limited set of right answers. A creative team who has thoughtfully considered each step of the framework will arrive at a musical solution that is effective for the scene. Similarly, the framework helps decision-makers avoid ineffective answers. Should a creative team appropriately consider the time period of the plot, they would not choose contemporary jazz for a medieval drama. Should a creative team appropriately match the emotion of the music with the emotion of the scene, they would not choose upbeat circus music for a serious love scene. Following the framework allows the creative team to eliminate objectively ineffective solutions.

Nonetheless, a certain amount of subjectivity arises within the set of potential right answers. Complicating the task, the creative team must make a singular choice. Each scene can have only one piece of music. Often, the process of selecting that one piece of music leads to debate among the creative team. Most commonly, differences of opinion arise when different individuals emphasize different factors in their decision-making process. For instance, it could be that a producer desires a musical style that will appeal to the film's target demographic. The director may prefer a different style that is similar to a previous film. The composer may prefer yet another style that reflects the story's geographical location. All of these opinions are legitimate, but they lead to different outcomes.

In such situations, creative professionals need to communicate openly and honestly, simultaneously expressing their viewpoint while listening to others. Most frequently, each point of view has some merit and should be considered before a final decision is made. In these cases, the framework can be used to facilitate the discussion. The framework helps team members pinpoint exactly where opinions diverge. After pinpointing the exact difference of opinion, team members can discuss the options openly and build consensus around a single solution.

CHAPTER 3

Style

The next series of chapters each discuss one of the dimensions of the framework. We start with musical style.

Determining the musical style of a score is one of the most fundamental decisions the creative team must make. Musically, there is no shortage of options. Orchestral music, hip-hop, rock 'n' roll, jazz, world music, period music—nearly every style of music has been used in a film at some point. In this chapter, we will discuss factors that should be considered when determining the musical style of a full score or individual scene.

GEOGRAPHICAL LOCATION

In most cases, the geographical location of the story will greatly impact the style of music desired for a scene or score. Specific countries, cities, and continents have their own musical heritage, and incorporating unique ideas from these traditions can reinforce the setting of the film.

Slumdog Millionaire (Fox Searchlight, 2008) tells the story of a boy from a poor neighborhood of Mumbai who answers every question correctly on the Indian version of *Who Wants to Be a Millionaire?* The soundtrack, composed by A. R. Rahman, incorporates traditional Indian instrumentation with present day Indian pop music and synthesizers.

Crouching Tiger, Hidden Dragon (Sony Classics, 2000) tells a story of love and combat amongst warriors during the Qing Dynasty. The music, composed by Tan Dun, incorporates orchestra, Asian percussion, ethnic flutes, and cello solos performed with ornamentation and glissandos typical of Asian musical styles.

In both of these cases, the stylistic choices in the music reinforce the geographical location of the film. The locations—India and China—have rich musical traditions that offer relatively specific choices for the composer. Namely, instrumentation and melodic scales specific to the location of the film can be incorporated into the music.

In some films, the geographical location of the plot is fictional or hypothetical. In such situations, the creative team has a great deal of artistic license and can speculate what kind of music would be associated with the fictional setting.

Avatar (Twentieth Century Fox, 2009) tells the story of space travelers who journey to the distant world Pandora, which is rich in natural resources and inhabited by a race called the Na'vi. The Na'vi live a hunter-gatherer lifestyle in the jungle and employ primitive weapons and tools. Given that the Na'vi are a fictional society, the exact sound of their musical tradition is pure speculation for the filmmakers and audience. The score, composed by James Horner, incorporates primal drums, flutes, and vocals intended to match the primitive appearance of the Na'vi. The world music elements are general in nature, meaning they are not immediately associated with a specific culture here on earth. By avoiding instrumentation specific to societies here on earth, the music does not immediately suggest Indian, Peruvian, or other earthbound society. Instead, it could conceivably be a musical heritage unique to the Na'vi.

Atlantis: The Lost Empire (Walt Disney Feature Animation, 2001) tells the story of explorers searching for the sunken city of Atlantis. Upon locating the city, the explorers are surprised to find it inhabited. The score, composed by James Newton Howard, includes musical themes associated with the people of Atlantis. For instrumentation, these themes combine traditional orchestra with gamelan instrumentation. Gamelan is a musical tradition from the Java and Bali islands of Indonesia. While one could never know what musical traditions would exist in the mythical sunken city of Atlantis, one might speculate it could be similar to the musical traditions of Pacific Island nations.

When emulating geographical location, there is often a divide between urban and rural locations. Contemporary musical styles, such as hip-hop and rock, are associated with urban locations. Traditional musical styles, such as orchestral music and styles exclusively using acoustic instruments, are associated with rural locations.

Fight Club (Twentieth Century Fox, 1999) tells the story of a depressed insomniac who builds a network of underground fighting clubs. *Fight Club* is set in an unspecified urban location, with most scenes occurring in bars, skyscrapers, and dilapidated urban neighborhoods. The score, composed by the Dust Brothers, utilizes contemporary beats and synthesizers, all processed heavily with distortion and effects.

Brokeback Mountain (Focus Features, 2005) tells the love story of two cowboys who meet as sheep herders on a Wyoming ranch. The score, composed by Gustavo Santaolalla, incorporates country style guitar and orchestral strings. The score is supplemented with country songs by artists such as Willy Nelson.

In all of the above cases, the geographical location of the story had a direct impact of the style of music in the film. By basing the musical style on the location of the plot, the music feels highly customized to the project and reinforces the location of the film for the audience.

LOCATION IN TIME

In most cases, the time period location of the story will greatly impact the style of music desired for a scene or score. Specific decades and centuries have their own musical style and incorporating ideas specific to these eras can reinforce the setting of the film.

The impact of time on a soundtrack could not be demonstrated more clearly than in a movie about time travel. The story of *Back to the Future* (Universal Studios, 1985) begins in 1985. The beginning of the film features the song "Power of Love," a single by Huey Lewis and the News. "Power of Love" is in the style of 1980s popular music and reached number 1 on the U.S. *Billboard* charts after the release of the film. Also at the beginning of the film, the single "Time Bomb Town" is heard playing from a clock radio. "Time Bomb Town" was written in 1985 by Lindsey Buckingham, the lead guitarist of Fleetwood Mac. Both "Power of Love" and "Time Bomb Town" help place the initial setting of the film in 1985.

As the film progresses, the main character Marty McFly boards a time machine invented by the eccentric Dr. Emmett Brown and travels back in time to 1955. Shortly after arrival in 1955, Marty walks through the town square of his hometown Hill Valley. At this point, the soundtrack shifts to a 1954 recording of "Mr. Sandman," performed by the Four Aces. Marty stumbles into a nearby café, where a 1954 recording of "The Ballad of Davy Crockett" is playing on the jukebox. Both recordings help establish the change in setting from 1985 to 1955.

At the end of the film, Marty successfully returns to 1985 in the time machine. When the setting shifts back to 1985, "Heaven is One Step Away" is heard playing on the radio of a homeless person in the park. "Heaven Is One Step Away" was recorded in 1985 by Eric Clapton. After Marty gets a much needed night of sleep, he awakens to his clock radio playing "Back in Time" by Huey Lewis and the News, also a popular hit in 1985. Both "Heaven Is One Step Away" and "Back in Time" establish the change in setting from 1955 back to 1985.

In the case of *Back to the Future*, popular songs from different eras are used to establish changes in the time period location of the plot. The technique can also be incorporated in a film's instrumental score and in films that take place in a single time period.

Sense and Sensibility (Columbia Pictures, 1995) details the love interests of the Dashwood family, which faces a change in financial standing after the passing of the family patriarch. Based on the 1811 novel by Jane Austin, the film is set in England in the 1790s. The score, composed by Patrick Doyle, draws heavily upon European classical music from the late 1700s. The instrumentation emphasizes strings, woodwinds, harp, and piano, all prominent in the music of classical composers such as Haydn and Mozart. The score includes songs for soprano performed in classical operatic style. By contrast, the score makes limited use of percussion and brass, which became more prominent in the romantic era of the 1800s, and entirely avoids contemporary instrumentation such as synthesizers and electric guitar. In this case, the stylistic choices in the score help to reinforce the time period location of the plot.

With films set in the past and present, the music can draw upon known musical styles to reinforce the time period. By contrast, the musical styles of future time periods can't be known to present day filmmakers, giving the creative team more flexibility with films set in the future. Nonetheless, the most common choice is to associate the most recent musical developments in popular music with future time periods.

The Matrix (Warner Brothers, 1999) tells the story of Neo, a computer programmer and hacker who leads a revolution among a future generation of humans enslaved by artificially intelligent machines. The exact time period of the plot is unknown, though the character Morpheus speculates the year is approximately 2199. The music incorporates a series of edgy rock songs that utilize electric guitar, electric bass, synthesizers, drum kit, rhythmic loops, aggressive vocals, and electronically processed effects on various instruments. Stylistically, the music is a forward looking projection of recent musical developments such as the use of electronic instruments and distortion, taking those developments to an extreme.

The Orchestra

At this point, a special note should be made about the use of the orchestra in film music. Historically, the orchestra evolved into its current form in Europe during the eighteenth and nineteenth century. Given the previous discussion, one might expect the orchestra to be associated solely with that time period and location.

However, orchestral music has been used throughout the history of film to convey the emotions of the story regardless of the setting of the plot. *Troy* (Warner Brothers, 2004) is set in ancient Greece at approximately 1200 B.C. The film features an orchestral score by James Horner. By contrast, the various films and television series of *Star Trek* take place in the distant future, predominantly during the twenty-second, twenty-third, and twenty-fourth centuries. Each *Star Trek* project also uses an orchestral score.

Because of repeated use in all time periods and locations, the sound of the orchestra now transcends time and place for film audiences.

STYLE OF SIMILAR PROJECTS

When determining the style of music for a project, the stylistic choices in other similar projects weigh heavily on decisions made by the creative team. Most projects can be described in general stylistic terms—an action adventure film, animated feature, romantic comedy, sports highlights television show, and so on. In each of these cases, a certain style of music is associated with the genre at large. For a new project within a given genre, the creative team must decide if their project will stylistically emulate or diverge from previous films in that genre.

Raiders of the Lost Ark (Paramount, 1981) is the first in a series of films detailing the adventures of Indiana Jones, who travels the world seeking treasure, solving mysteries, overcoming obstacles, and defeating foes. Each Indiana Jones film to date has used an orchestral score by John Williams. The scores feature a heroic theme associated with the main character and other memorable themes linked to specific characters and plot situations. The scores use the traditional orchestra while occasionally incorporating world music elements based on the location of the latest adventure.

The Indiana Jones films are some of the most successful action adventure films ever made. As such, they set a stylistic standard for the genre and present a question to every producer, director, and composer working on a new action adventure film. Should the music in the new film use techniques similar to those used in the Indiana Jones films?

The answer to this question is ultimately a matter of personal preference for the creative team of the new project. Often, the choice comes down to a balance between the creative team's desire to be different and their comfort level with risk. Emulating previous projects reduces risk. When a project has a similar production budget, marketing budget, and stylistic approach to a previous film, the studio will hope that the two projects will perform similarly at the box office. Diverging from techniques established by previous projects increases the level of risk. When a project is genuinely unique, it is harder for a studio to forecast how it will do financially because there is no precedent on which to base a forecast.

All film industry professionals desire to be creative. However, as the financial implications of a project rise, the pressure to ensure a successful project increases. Making choices that are viewed as different exposes the creative team to criticism in the event the project underperforms. Of course, when a project blazes a new path creatively and is wildly successful at the box office, the creative team is heralded as heroic visionaries.

Ultimately, there is no single answer to this question, but every creative team on every project must make a choice between emulating or diverging from previous projects in the genre. Those making an action adventure film that wish to remain within the traditions of the genre will seek an orchestral score in the style of an Indiana Jones score. Those making an action adventure film that wish to do something different will specifically avoid an orchestral score in the style of an Indiana Jones score.

Notably, in the case of a sequel or film franchise, the decision is nearly always to emulate the previous film. In each of the Indiana Jones films, John Williams was hired as the composer and an orchestral score was created utilizing the musical theme from the original *Raiders of the Lost Ark*. Typically, the goal of a sequel or franchise is to capitalize on the success and established brand of the initial film. In such a scenario, a significant departure from the style of the original film is rarely desired.

That said, subtle variation from film to film within a franchise can be desirable and effective. *Alien* (Twentieth Century Fox, 1979) details how an alien life form gets aboard a commercial ship and terrorizes the crew. The film is predominantly about suspense and fear, as the crew attempts to survive their encounter with an entirely unknown life form. The alien itself is rarely shown in the film and encounters with it are brief but deadly. The musical score by Jerry Goldsmith matches this suspenseful style, utilizing dissonant harmonies and creepy effects in predominantly sustained textures.

The sequel *Aliens* (Twentieth Century Fox, 1986) incorporates a great deal more high-energy action and battle footage, as a group of marines travels to the alien's home moon to investigate. The stylistic shift is immediately apparent from the *Aliens* movie poster, which stated "This Time, It's War." The musical score by James Horner matches this stylistic shift, incorporating larger instrumentation, militaristic percussion, and high-energy rhythmic patterns.

DISTRIBUTION CHANNEL

When determining the style of music for a project, the ultimate distribution channel for the project can impact the style of music desired. The impact of a defined distribution channel is perhaps clearest with television networks. Often, a given television network will have a stylistic preference that will impact the musical choices across all of their shows. As a result, it's not uncommon for two separate networks to have shows based on a similar plot premise, but the music will sound different from network to network.

In film, which studio is funding the project can have an impact on the stylistic direction of the music. In many cases, studios have had past success with a certain style and seek to replicate that style in future projects.

Snow White and the Seven Dwarfs (Walt Disney Productions, 1937) tells the story of a kindhearted princess who is bewitched by an evil and jealous queen. Snow White is rescued by her true love, Prince Charming, who lifts the curse with a kiss. The story is told in animation, depicting Snow White interacting with forest animals and singing dwarves. Musically, the film uses an orchestral score and occasional songs performed with orchestral accompaniment. *Snow White* was very successful at the box office in 1937 and, when adjusted for inflation, remains one of the highest grossing films of all time.

Since *Snow White*, Disney Animation has created a series of films that use a similar stylistic approach. Animation is used to tell a story that would be impossible to tell with live action, including forest animals that interact with humans and inanimate objects such as kitchenware that come to life and sing. Musically, the story is enhanced with an orchestral score and songs that place vocals above predominantly orchestral accompaniment. This basic stylistic approach is the foundation of Disney animated features from *Snow White* in 1937 to *Beauty and the Beast* (Walt Disney Feature Animation) in 1991 and *Frozen* (Walt Disney Animation Studios) in 2013. Remaining within this style on future projects both capitalizes on the success of past projects and strengthens the value of Disney Animation as a brand.

By contrast, animated features made by different studios may consciously diverge from this precedent. *Shrek* (DreamWorks, 2001) tells the story of an ogre and princess who fall in love. On the surface, the film has similarities to Disney films—there is a talking donkey and ogre. A fire-breathing dragon guards a princess in a castle. However, the story ends with a surprising twist. Rather than true love turning the ugly ogre into a handsome prince, true love turns the beautiful princess into an ogre. The two ogres then live happily ever after. Musically, the film also diverges from the precedent set by Disney films. Rather than using traditional songs with orchestral accompaniment, the songs in *Shrek* are rock songs such as "All Star" by Smash Mouth and Leonard Cohen's "Hallelujah," performed for the movie by John Cale. These songs are produced in a contemporary style, using electric guitar, bass, keyboards, drum set, and vocals. Likely, these choices were made to differentiate *Shrek* from the Disney films—because *Shrek* was made by DreamWorks rather than Disney.

When deciding on the stylistic direction of the music for a project, the creative team should take into consideration the stylistic precedent set by that television network or film studio. Networks and studios represent a continuum of thought, a historical progression of creative decisions made from project to project. Most often, networks and studios wish to take the next logical step in their continuum of thought while simultaneously differentiating themselves from stylistic choices made by other networks and studios.

TARGET DEMOGRAPHIC

When determining the style of music for a project, the target demographic can be factored into the decisions by the creative team. A demographic is a limited subset of the overall potential film audience. Demographics are commonly segmented by gender and age, such as men, women, children, teenagers, adults, or other groups. With most films, the producers have an idea of what demographic they want the film to appeal to, and this goal underlies all creative decisions.

Superbad (Columbia Pictures, 2007) tells the story of several high school aged boys who attempt to attend parties, acquire alcohol, and win the affections of girls. The plot is clearly tailored towards the teenage demographic, staring young actors whose characters are placed in situations most relevant to high school aged students. The soundtrack to *Superbad* licensed songs from popular music styles with a particular emphasis on '60s–'70s funk. Lyle Workman, who is a composer, guitarist, and music producer working in popular music styles, composed the score. The score was recorded with several all-star musicians from the funk scene, including Bootsy Collins, Bernie Worrell, John "Jabo" Starks, Clyde Stubblefield, and Phelps "Catfish" Collins. Given the teenage target demographic, using music from popular music styles rather than an orchestral score was an appropriate stylistic choice. The focus on funk serves the comedic purposes of the film—using a super cool James Brown-esque sound to accompany several awkward teenagers trying so hard to be cool.

The Green Mile (Warner Brothers, 1999) tells the story of prison guards who work a death row penitentiary in the 1930s. They encounter an inmate with supernatural capabilities and ultimately realize that he is an innocent man. The death row story is told as a flashback by the prison guard supervisor, who is now a 108-year-old man living in a retirement home. *The Green Mile* is a film that targets an older adult demographic. All of the characters in the film are adults, and large portions of the plot take place in a retirement home. The film addresses serious topics such as death and outliving your loved ones. Musically, the film uses an orchestral score by Thomas Newman. The score is supplemented by songs from the 1930s such as "Cheek to Cheek" performed by Fred Astaire and "I Can't Give You Anything But Love" by Billie Holiday. While these songs help reinforce the time period setting of the film, they also appeal to the older demographic that is the target audience.

With most films, every creative decision on the project is made with a target demographic in mind. The creative team should be aware of this when determining musical direction and choose musical styles that will appeal to the target demographic.

BUDGET

The budget of a project will have an impact on the style of music that can be used on a film. Large budget projects offer creative freedom for the creative teams. When the budget is sufficient, the producer can hire a famous composer and record a score with a full orchestra. If the project includes a large licensing budget, a music supervisor can approach record labels about licensing well-known popular songs.

When the budget is more limited, some stylistic options become more practical than others. Styles that can be produced in a studio by a single composer/producer are inherently less expensive than styles that require many musicians. As such, a score using synthesizers and beats is less expensive to produce than a full orchestral score.

In addition, the desire for very unique musical styles can require a larger music budget. There are a large number of music libraries that offer prerecorded music for use in films. Music libraries offer music in a wide variety of styles at a low cost. However, when the stylistic preference is very specific—such as a hybrid score that combines gamelan and orchestral instrumentation—it becomes more difficult to find prerecorded music that meets these specifications. Projects that require a specific and unique musical style often require hiring a composer and recording new music.

In order to stay on budget, low budget projects use music that can be acquired inexpensively. Stylistically, this means an extensive use of synthesizer and software-based music, as well as styles readily available in large quantities from music libraries. Ultimately, the creative team must factor budget into their stylistic choice, identifying a musical solution that meets the dramatic needs of the film while staying within the film's music budget.

HYBRID STYLES VS. ALTERNATING CUES

Many films have more than one style of music in the film. When incorporating multiple styles in a soundtrack, the creative team has two general options. First, the music can alternate styles from cue to cue. One cue will be in one style, another cue will be in another style. As an example from a film we've already discussed, *Back to the Future* takes this approach. The soundtrack includes '50s rock 'n' roll, '80s pop music, and an orchestral score by Alan Silvestri. For the most part, these styles remain separate, with the music being limited to one style at a time. Second, a composer can create new music that merges characteristics of two styles. The score to *Atlantis: The Lost Empire* includes music that merges gamelan and orchestral instrumentation.

Whether to create a hybrid score or alternate styles from cue to cue is a subjective decision to be made by the creative team on each project. Many projects could be scored successfully with either approach. Nonetheless, the two approaches have different strengths and weaknesses. Alternating between distinct musical styles works particularly well when there are frequent changes in location and time period. As we saw with *Back to the Future*, music from different time periods is used to reinforce the changes in time location in the plot. Had these been hybrid cues that blended multiple musical styles, that would have weakened the impact of the music. In addition, alternating between musical styles is the most practical solution for projects that use a significant amount of licensed music. While virtually every musical style is available for licensing from a music library or record label, music that effectively merges two disparate styles is in less supply.

By contrast, a hybrid score can be effective when the location and time period are comparatively stable. *Braveheart* (Paramount, 1995) takes place in the thirteenth and fourteenth centuries. It tells the story of William Wallace, a Scotsman who leads a fight for independence from the English. The film uses a score by James Horner that combines traditional orchestral instrumentation with uilleann pipes. The large orchestral instrumentation makes the music feel like a cinematic Hollywood film score, while the bagpipes help set the location in the British Isles.

CHOOSING A STYLISTIC DIRECTION

Selecting a musical style for the project is one of the most important decisions in making a film. It is also a difficult decision that includes a certain amount of subjectivity. Should the music incorporate instrumentation specific to the geographical location of the plot? Should the music sound different from or similar to other projects in the genre? The optimal answers to these questions vary from project to project and ultimately depend on a certain degree of personal opinion among members of the creative team.

A creative professional's goal should be to develop a systematic process for identifying all possible stylistic choices and then make a selection they believe best supports the film. With the goal of systematic decision-making in mind, this book includes an appendix with a variety of worksheets. The "Style Determination" worksheet is a series of questions focused on musical style. Early on in a project, the creative team can use the worksheet to identify the factors that may impact musical style. After answering each question in the worksheet, decision-makers will be well positioned to make a choice they believe to be right for the film.

Notably, musical style can vary throughout a film, particularly in projects with frequent changes in time period and geographical location. In such films, the worksheet can be used on a scene-by-scene basis.

Characteristics of Musical Style

Once a musical style has been selected, it becomes the composer's job to create a musical score within that style. In the case of projects that license preexisting music, it's the music supervisor's job to find music within the desired style. Typically, composers and music supervisors are trained musicians who have spent a great deal of time studying various musical styles. Such study is a matter of basic survival for composers and music supervisors working in film and television. A composer is frequently asked to switch styles, writing hip-hop one day and orchestral music the next day. Music supervisors are asked to find music in a wide variety of styles and must be knowledgeable about any music that could potentially be used in film.

Identifying the key characteristics of a given style can be a complicated task. Typically, a complex combination of instrumentation, harmonic progressions, melodic scales, recording techniques, performance techniques, and other musical characteristics combine to give a style its characteristic sound. Complicating the task is the fact that the defining characteristic varies from style to style. In some cases, the instrumentation is the defining characteristic. In other cases, the melodic scale is the defining characteristic. And so on.

The process of studying any style begins with listening to examples characteristic of the style. While you listen, critically analyze every aspect of the music. The "Style Characteristics" worksheet in the appendix is designed for this purpose. The goal is to identify the instrumentation, harmony, melody, rhythm, form, performance techniques, and recording techniques used in a high percentage of examples in the style.

As one example, figure 3.1 completes "Style Characteristics" for classical chamber music.

STYLE CHARACTERISTICS

Style Name: Classical Chamber Music

Instrumentation

Overall Instrumentation: Small instrumentation. Typically 1–5 players.

Melodic Instrumentation: Varies, but frequently in upper register.

Harmony

Scale Type: Major and Minor Scales

Chord Types: Usually triads and seventh chords

Common Progressions: Tonic » Pre-dominant » Dominant » Tonic

Common Modulations (or lack thereof): Modulations to Dominant or Subdominant

Harmonic Rhythm: Typically faster than film music

Melody

Common Melodic Intervals: Varies, but mostly remains within the scale

Melodic Phrasing: Varies, but 4-, 8-, and 16-bar phrases are common

Rhythm

Meter: Commonplace meters such as 3/4, 4/4, 9/8, and 12/8.

Beat Subdivision: Duple and Triple

Tempo: Varies

Common Rhythms: Varies

Miscellaneous

Form: Classical forms such as Sonata form and Rondo form

Compositional Structure: Varies

Performance Techniques: Traditional

Recording Techniques: Traditional

FIG. 3.1. Style Characteristics for Classical Chamber Music

Classical chamber music was written for small instrumentation, such as string quartet (two violins, viola, and cello) or piano trio (violin, cello, and piano). Typically, all instruments got a chance to play the melody, though it was most frequently placed in the highest pitched element. The most common scale types were major and minor scales. Chords were typically triads and seventh chords built from the pitches of the scale. Modulations occurred frequently, most commonly to the dominant and subdominant key. The music used classical forms such as sonata form and rondo form. In film scoring, classical chamber music is used to elicit European society in the eighteenth and nineteenth centuries.

While completing the worksheet, special note should be made of any characteristics that are unique to that style, meaning they rarely appear in other styles. For instance, the didgeridoo is an instrument used in indigenous Australian music but rarely appears in other musical styles. Harpsichord is a keyboard instrument common in the baroque era of classical music that then fell out of favor in the classical and romantic eras. Any instrument or characteristic that is specific to a single musical style is particularly useful, as the audience will immediately associate that sound with the relevant style. When the audience hears a didgeridoo, they immediately think of the Australian outback. When the audience hears a harpsichord, they think of baroque-era Europe.

When studying musical styles, recognize that there will always be examples that are typical of a given style and other examples that are atypical for a given style. In some cases, the atypical example will be so unusual as to create confusion—is it within the style at all? Or is your definition of the style incorrect?

Begin by defining the most typical characteristics for that style. By initially focusing on the most typical examples, you can draw concrete conclusions about the style. Moreover, the most typical example defines the initial reference point for both the audience and creative team. If the musical style is a rock song, the expectation is likely a vocal melody with harmonic accompaniment in guitar, keyboards, bass, and drum set. Of course, there are atypical examples that are entirely instrumental, such as "The Ox" by The Who. Nonetheless, this atypical example does not change the expectation that "rock songs" utilize vocals.

After clearly defining the most typical characteristics of a style, making note of exceptions and atypical examples can be creatively interesting and informative. Atypical examples can be artistically beautiful. In some cases, defying the listener's expectations is the most effective creative choice. In the instance of music for film, the question of whether to use music typical or atypical of a given style is a simple extension of the initial selection of a musical style. Ultimately, the composer or music supervisor must make this decision in close consultation with the full creative team.

CHAPTER 4

Emotion

One of the primary roles of music in film is to enhance the audience's emotional experience. For the creative team addressing this issue, the central question is simple. What should the audience feel? While this seems to be a straight-forward question, the question can lead to significant debate. For an intense battle scene, the primary emotion could be fear, adrenaline, heroism, triumph, despair, or doom. Ultimately, a creative team who answers this question with clarity and consensus has taken a significant step towards designing an effective musical score.

ENHANCE THE STORY

The creative team should begin by determining what emotions exist in the story even without music. The role of the music is then to enhance those emotions. When the scene is scary without music, the music should make it scarier. When the scene is happy without music, the music should make it happier. This is a markedly different goal than having the music change the emotional content of a story. For instance, the music should not take a sad scene and make it funny. It is not the role of the music to impose its will on the story. Rather, the music should follow the lead of the story, taking the emotions inherent in the story and intensifying them.

The score to *Jaws* (Universal Pictures, 1975) effectively intensifies the emotions of the story. The film is set in a fictional New England resort town during peak summer holiday season. A great white shark terrorizes local beach-goers, attacking several swimmers and causing multiple deaths. Local police chief Martin Brody, oceanographer Matt Hooper, and professional shark hunter Quint set to the sea to hunt the shark. In the 81st minute of the film, Brody is chumming the water with chopped fish to attract the shark. Everything seems normal, and then the shark suddenly lunges out of the water at the back of the boat. Brody, shocked and startled, stumbles backwards and mutters to Quint, "You're going to need a bigger boat."

Emotionally, the scene begins with neutral ambivalence. The characters bicker about who is in charge and who should complete dirty tasks such as chumming the water. Out of this ambivalence comes shock and surprise. Seemingly out of nowhere, the shark suddenly lunges at the boat. After the initial surprise, fear and terror set in as the characters contemplate the massive size of the shark.

The score, composed by John Williams, takes all of these emotions and turns them up a notch. As Brody is chumming the water, there is no music. Music here is unnecessary as the emotions are vague and muted. In addition, music at this point would lessen the surprise to come, a decidedly undesirable outcome. When the shark suddenly lunges out of the water, the full orchestra comes in equally suddenly. By going from no music to a fortissimo hit, the music makes the surprise more surprising. As Brody stumbles backward, tremolo strings perform chromatic lines and dissonant harmonies—compositional ideas that produce fear and terror in listeners. All of these emotions—ambivalence, shock, and terror—are inherent in the story. The music takes these emotions and makes them more intense.

THE PROTAGONIST AND ANTAGONIST

The creative team's ultimate concern is the emotional response of the audience. Of course, the audience's emotions are frequently aligned with the experiences of sympathetic characters in the film. As such, the creative team should identify whether or not the audience holds a sympathetic view of each character.

The *protagonist* is the main character of the story. Most fundamentally, the story is about experiences had by the protagonist. In the vast majority of films, the audience holds a sympathetic view of the protagonist. The audience is upset when something bad happens to the protagonist and pleased when something good happens.

The *antagonist* is the character set in opposition to the protagonist. The antagonist creates obstacles and challenges for the protagonist. Accordingly, the audience is unsympathetic to the antagonist. The audience is upset when something good happens to the antagonist and pleased when something bad happens.

In *The Lion King* (Walt Disney Feature Animation, 1994), the protagonist is Simba. Simba begins the film as a lion cub, heir to the king of the jungle. The antagonist is Simba's wicked uncle Scar. Scar plots to take the throne by killing Simba and his father Mufasa. First, he lures Simba into the path of a wildebeest stampede. Mufasa dies in an attempt to rescue Simba. Last, Scar convinces Simba that he is responsible for Mufasa's death, and Simba flees in exile. In the 40th minute of the film, Scar ascends to the throne. For the audience, the moment is upsetting and traumatic. The evil villain has triumphed. The music, composed by Hans Zimmer, enhances these emotions, using a minor key, march-like rhythms in the strings, and a dramatic build from small instrumentation to full orchestra.

At the end of the film, Simba returns from exile to find his homeland desolate and burnt. Simba confronts Scar. After the two lions fight, Simba leaves a wounded Scar in the hands of a pack of ravenous hyenas. In the 81st minute of the film, Simba ascends to the throne. The sun comes out and the jungle returns to life. For the audience, the moment is cathartic and triumphant. The music modulates to a major key, a choir enters, and large percussion accents important beats. The score then transitions to the film's upbeat anthem "Circle of Life."

In both of these scenes, a lion is ascending to the throne as king of the jungle. However, the audience's emotional response to the scenes differs drastically. In the first scene, the antagonist is ascending to the throne and the audience experiences starkly negative emotions. In the second scene, the protagonist is ascending to the throne and the audience experiences positive emotions.

All films contain secondary characters that are neither the protagonist nor the antagonist. Nonetheless, the audience can have strong feelings for the secondary characters. In *The Lion King*, Nala, Zazu, Timon, and Pumba are all sympathetic characters that the audience relates to and cares about. The hyenas Shenzi, Banzai, and Ed are antagonistic characters of which the audience holds a negative view. In any given scene, the experiences and actions of these characters may contribute significantly to the audience's emotional response.

In this film, the emotional positioning of each character is comparatively straightforward. Simba is a clear-cut protagonist. Scar is a clear-cut antagonist. Some films present more ambiguous scenarios, such as a protagonist who has notable character flaws. Such films can require different musical solutions.

Heat (Warner Brothers, 1995) is a high-stakes crime drama pitting a police detective against a professional thief. Despite using a thief and detective as main characters, *Heat* does not portray a clear-cut protagonist or antagonist. Both the thief and detective display a combination of virtuous and flawed characteristics. Throughout the film, the two characters are shown to be more similar than different. At one point, the two even sit down for coffee and have a respectful conversation. At the end of the film, the detective kills the thief in a shootout. The moment is not a climactic conquest of good over evil, but rather the inevitable outcome of two determined characters set in opposition. The music, composed by Elliot Goldenthal, reflects the lack of a protagonist and antagonist. Rather than stating clear hero and villain themes, the score focuses on drama and suspense. During the final shooting scene, synthesizers sustain a dramatic low pedal point. A minor key melody is layered on top in the mid-register.

Another complex scenario occurs when multiple sympathetic characters experience different emotions. One such scene occurs at the climax of *The Green Mile*. Both the prison inmate John Coffey and guard supervisor Paul Hedgecomb are sympathetic characters. John, despite being an innocent man, has been convicted of murder and is on death row. Once the prison guards realize he is innocent, Paul asks John what his wishes are. John explains that he is weary from years of witnessing humanity's crimes, and he could obtain peace if the execution were to continue. During the execution scene, the prison guards experience confusion and sadness. Their job requires completing the execution, and John has asked for the execution to continue. Nonetheless, they believe John to be an innocent man who uses his supernatural talents to help people. John is also experiencing mixed emotions. He is experiencing fear while hoping to achieve a final peace. In addition, the room is filled with spectators who believe John is a murderer. The spectators are filled with anger and hatred. Amidst this stew of complex emotions, Thomas Newman scored the scene with emotional music that utilizes a variety of harmonies. The chords shift between minor and major, underscoring both the sadness and hope of the scene. The instrumentation includes sustained strings, piano, and occasional woodwinds. The tempo is slow, and the texture is sustained.

WHAT DOES THE AUDIENCE KNOW

At all times, the creative team should keep in mind what the audience does and does not know. The emotional response the audience has in a scene is based on the information currently available to the audience. While the creative team knows what will happen in the next scene and at the end of the film, the audience does not. When making decisions about emotion, the creative team should ignore the events to come in the future and base their decisions on the audience's current access to information.

Monsters, Inc. (Pixar Animation, 2001) tells the story of employees at Monsters Incorporated. Monsters Incorporated is an energy company located in Monstropolis, a bustling city of monsters. Monsters Incorporated produces energy by harnessing the screams of human children. The monsters sneak into children's bedrooms at night, scare them, and harvest the screams. Despite their ominous job description, not all the monsters are villains. The heroes of the film, Mike and Sully, are fun, loveable, and funny monsters.

The main title sequence is a series of moving colorful doors, giving the audience only a tangential hint of the coming story. Following the main title, the audience sees a young boy sleeping comfortably in bed. The boy looks at his closet and sees the door left open. In the darkness, the hanging clothes rustle in an unnatural way. Next, a monster emerges and looms over the boy, casting an ominous shadow across the bed. The boy screams.

At this point, the audience believes the human boy is real and terrified of the monster. The audience naturally relates to the human boy and assumes the monster to be the villain. Accordingly, the audience feels fear and terror. The music, composed by Randy Newman, intensifies these emotions. The music uses orchestral instrumentation and dissonant harmonies. It starts softly and builds to a dissonant climax as the monster looms over the boy.

Just after the boy screams, the full truth is revealed to the audience. The boy is not real, but rather is an animatronic robot. The monster is not particularly scary and is actually terrified of the child. After the animatronic boy screams, the monster screams even louder, trips over toys, and falls to the floor. Next, an alarm goes off and lights turn on. A classroom and instructor are revealed, showing this is all a training exercise at Monsters Incorporated. All of this information was unknown to the audience just seconds ago, as they felt fear for a helpless boy being terrorized by an ominous monster. As the full story is revealed, the scary music abruptly stops and the dialogue drives the scene.

In some cases, the information the audience has diverges from the perspective of the on-screen characters. In such cases, the music should continue to score the scene from the perspective of the audience. The opening scene from *Monsters, Inc.* also demonstrates this concept. From the perspective of the characters, the monster is a mild-mannered employee at a training exercise. From the audience's, the monster is a scary beast threatening a boy. The music is scored from the audience's perspective.

There is one noteworthy exception to the above guideline: a case in which the music should be scored from the perspective of the on-screen characters. The exception to the rule is a satirical gag in a comedy. Imagine a scene in which two elderly men compete in a race. Both men use walkers and progress at a very slow pace. Nonetheless, the men take the race very seriously, competing with focus and determination. In this situation, there is a divergence between the perspective of the characters and the audience. The characters believe it's a serious high-speed dash, while the audience believes it is a silly snail's pace walk. In a comedy, the scene is funniest when scored from the perspective of the characters. The music could be an Olympic fanfare or high-energy action cue. In the case of a comedic gag, scoring the scene from the perspective of the characters enhances the humor.

STUDYING EMOTION IN MUSIC

Emotion is an inherently abstract concept, making it difficult to discuss and study. For the creative team, discussing emotion in a concrete manner is simultaneously challenging and beneficial.

Both musicians and non-musicians should brainstorm adjectives that describe common emotions in film—love, sadness, fear, heroism, adventure, and so on. "Analyzing Emotion" in the appendix is intended for this purpose. Identifying the emotional content of a scene with a specific word helps the creative team communicate to one another and build consensus.

For the musicians working in film, turning these emotions into specific musical ideas is a fundamental component of the job. Every composer and music supervisor should aim to accumulate a "bag of tricks" based on each emotion. Composers can experiment within their own compositions, and all musicians can study emotion by analyzing existing pieces of music. Studying emotion is much like studying style: listen to a piece that elicits a given emotion, and identify the compositional characteristics of the music. Repeat this process with multiple pieces of music within each emotional genre. Specifically note any compositional ideas that occur repeatedly. Characteristics that appear repeatedly, when utilized in a new piece of music, are likely to produce that emotion in the listener.

"Studying Emotion in Music" in the appendix is intended for this purpose. As one example, figure 4.1 completes the "Studying Emotion in Music" worksheet for the emotion dark adventure.

STUDYING EMOTION IN MUSIC

Emotion: Dark Adventure

Instrumentation

Overall Instrumentation: Full Orchestra

Melodic Instrumentation: Varies, but frequent brass and low register melodic statements

Harmony

Scale Type: Minor scales or more chromatic

Chord Types: Minor triads and more dissonant

Common Progressions: Varies

Common Modulations: Modulations are common. Distant chromatic modulations are OK.

Harmonic Rhythm: Varies, but quick harmonic rhythm is common.

Melody

Common Melodic Intervals: Minor Seconds, Minor Thirds, Tritones

Melodic Phrasing: Clear prominent melodies. Frequently in 4-, 8-, and 16-bar phrases.

Rhythm

Meter: Commonplace meters. Typically 3/4, 4/4, 9/8, or 12/8.

Beat Subdivision: Duple or Triple

Tempo: Varies, but moderate tempo with quick subdivision is common.

Common Rhythms: Triplets and Dotted Rhythms

Miscellaneous

Form: Varies

Compositional Structure: Varies, but melody + countermelody + harmony is common

Performance Techniques: Traditional

Recording Techniques: Traditional

FIG. 4.1. Studying Emotion in Dark Adventure

Pieces from the classical repertoire that convey dark adventure include *Night on Bald Mountain* by Modest Mussorgsky and *The Sorcerer's Apprentice* by Paul Dukas. Dark adventure is commonly used in film when adventurers encounter ominous and dangerous situations. Dark adventure music typically uses full orchestral instrumentation with prominent contributions from brass and percussion. Low register melodic statements are common. The harmony is ominous, using minor keys, chromaticism, and dissonant chords. The melodies emphasize chromatic melodic intervals, particularly minor seconds, minor thirds, and tritones. Triplets and dotted rhythms—such as a dotted eighth note followed by a sixteenth note—are common. These characteristics, when incorporated into a new musical work, are likely to produce emotions of dark adventure.

CHAPTER 5

Energy Level

Energy level is the amount of musical and visual activity in the film. Most commonly, the creative team will choose music that matches and enhances the energy level of the visuals.

VISUAL ENERGY

The amount of energy in visual images is determined by several factors, including whether objects and characters in the picture are moving, whether the camera itself is stationary or moving, how frequently picture cuts occur, and what type of picture cuts are used.

Moving on-screen objects and characters, such as speeding cars and fighting soldiers, produce a high level of visual energy. The opening scene of *Star Wars Episode III: Revenge of the Sith* (Twentieth Century Fox, 2005) features a high-speed battle sequence. In the scene, Anakin Skywalker and Obi-Wan Kenobi pilot through a seemingly endless armada of dueling spacecraft. Visually, spacecraft fly across the screen at a high rate of speed, spacecraft perform spins and sudden changes in direction, objects explode and consume the image in flames, and ammunition launches from dueling spacecraft. Ultimately, Anakin and Obi-Wan crash-land their starfighters on the dock of a large enemy spacecraft. They quickly jump from their ships, draw their lightsabers, and duel battle droids amidst a flurry of laser fire. In the scene, objects and characters move quickly around the screen, creating high-energy visuals.

By contrast, the opening scene of *The Green Mile* employs slow motion to create low-energy visuals. In the scene, a group of men carrying rifles and pitchforks charge through a field. The group is on a manhunt, seeking a criminal who has kidnapped one of the men's daughters. In the middle of the scene, a man finds a piece of torn fabric on a shrub, inspects it, and yells to those following him. All of these visuals are placed in slow motion, dramatically reducing their visual energy. While the on-screen characters are moving, the audience experiences a low-energy floating effect due to the slow-motion technique.

Moving the vantage point of the camera can increase the visual energy. Moving camera effects include panning left or right, zooming in or out, or physically changing the location of the camera. Each effect changes the visual perspective for the audience, adds energy to stationary objects, and increases the energy of objects moving in contrary motion to the camera. The effect is seen noticeably in the opening scene of *Revenge of the Sith*. Throughout the battle, the physical location of the camera changes constantly. The camera flies alongside Anakin and Obi-Wan in their starfighters and moves in the opposite direction of explosions, debris, and spacecraft. As a result of the camera movement, otherwise stationary objects take on a great deal of visual energy and objects moving contrary to the camera have increased energy. In this scene, the moving camera dramatically increases the energy level of the visuals.

By contrast, the camera movement in the opening scene of *The Green Mile* is very subtle. The camera begins the scene in a stationary position. Next, the camera subtly pans to the right. In the last segment of the scene, the camera moves slowly to the audience's left while the characters run toward the left of the screen. In this case, the energy created by the camera movement is slight because the camera moves in parallel motion with the on-screen characters. In addition, the energy created by the camera movement is reduced by the slow-motion treatment. Overall, the subtlety of the camera movement contributes to the low-energy effect of the visuals.

The frequency of picture cuts will raise or lower the energy level of the visuals. A picture cut is a sudden change in the audience's vantage point. The image can move to a new location, show a different camera angle of the same event, or jump to a point in the future or past. The opening scene of *Revenge of the Sith* employs a large number of picture cuts. It begins with a long, single shot as the camera flies alongside Anakin's and Obi-Wan's starfighters, after which the picture cuts come fast and furious. In total, the opening scene includes over fifty picture cuts in the initial 3.5-minute battle sequence. The high frequency of picture cuts in the scene raises the energy level of the visuals.

By contrast, the opening scene of *The Green Mile* doesn't use any picture cuts. The scene is a single shot that slightly pans right and then gradually moves to the left. In this case, the absence of picture cuts contributes to the low energy level of the visuals.

The type of picture cuts used also impacts visual energy. Hard picture cuts that instantly change the image in a single frame are frequent in high-energy scenes. Slow crossfades, where one image gradually fades into another, are common in low-energy scenes. In the opening scene of *Revenge of the Sith*, every picture cut is a hard cut. In the opening scene of *The Green Mile*, there are no picture cuts within the scene. However, the scene begins with a gradual fade-in and ends with a gradual fade-out. In addition, text stating the film's title and production company overlays the image during the scene. Each text element gradually fades in and out.

The opening scenes of *Revenge of the Sith* and *The Green Mile* show how scenes can have different visual energy levels. The opening scene of *Revenge of the Sith* uses movement of on-screen objects and characters, movement of the camera itself, frequent picture cuts, and hard cuts to create a high visual energy level. The opening scene of *The Green Mile* uses little movement of on-screen objects and characters, slow camera movement, no picture cuts, and gradual fades to create a low visual energy level.

"Visual Energy Analysis" is provided in the appendix for analyzing the visual energy of a scene. Each question addresses a characteristic that impacts visual energy, after which an assessment of the overall energy can be made.

MUSICAL ENERGY

The overall energy level of music is determined by a variety of factors, including tempo, rhythmic subdivision of the beat, overall instrumentation, harmonic rhythm, and frequency of modulations.

Tempo is the speed at which a musical piece is performed. It is most commonly described in beats per minute. The beat is the primary pulse of the music—the speed at which listeners are most likely to tap their feet. An example of a slow tempo is 60 beats per minute, while an example of a fast tempo is 184 beats per minute.

The *rhythmic subdivision* of the beat is the fastest rhythmic unit played in the music. As one common example, the rhythmic subdivision of the beat is frequently played on hi-hats in a rock song, though any instrument might play a note that begins on a subdivision of the beat. Commonly, the rhythmic subdivision is two, three, or four subdivisions per beat. The pace of rhythmic subdivisions can range from nearly zero in sustained floating music up to approximately 500 per minute in fast driving music. In a high-energy action cue, the tempo may be 176 beats per minute and each beat has 3 subdivisions, creating 528 subdivisions per minute. In a low-energy love theme, the tempo may be 64 beats per minute with no more than 2 subdivisions per beat, creating 128 subdivisions per minute.

Together, the tempo and rhythmic subdivision determine the overall level of rhythmic activity in the music. In general, low-energy music has little rhythmic activity, created by a slow tempo with infrequent subdivisions of the beat. High-energy music has a great deal of rhythmic activity, created by a fast tempo with multiple subdivisions of the beat.

The overall size of the instrumentation contributes greatly to the energy level of the music. High-energy music is typically large in instrumentation. Low-energy music is typically small in instrumentation. What exactly constitutes large instrumentation will vary from style to style. For orchestral film music, large instrumentation entails the full woodwind family, full brass family, multiple layers of percussion, and the full string family. Often, choir is added to make the texture even larger. For other styles, the definition of large instrumentation will be different. For instance, sports rock typically includes electronic guitar, bass, keyboards, and multiple layers of percussion. Often, pop brass is added to make the texture even larger. Regardless of style, high-energy cues use all the instrumentation available in that style, while low-energy cues use some subset of the potential instrumentation.

In music theory, a chord is two or more notes played simultaneously. Collectively, all of the chords in a piece of music are referred to as the "harmony." The term "harmonic rhythm" refers to the pace at which chords change in music. Harmonic rhythm can play a significant role in determining the energy level of the music, with a faster harmonic rhythm creating a higher energy level. It is common for the chords to change once per measure, which is typically a group of three or four beats. A faster harmonic rhythm would be when the chords change every beat. A slower harmonic rhythm occurs when a single chord is used for an entire phrase, such as a group of eight measures.

The frequency with which modulations occur will raise or lower the energy level of the music. A modulation is a shift from one key to another. In music theory, a key includes two ingredients. First, the key specifies a single pitch as *tonic*—the most important pitch and the point of resolution. Second, the key specifies a scale, which is a group of pitches that is used to build the music. An example of a key is C major, which specifies C as tonic and uses a major scale. Likewise, D minor is a key that specifies D as tonic and uses a minor scale. A shift from C major to D minor, or from any key to another, is a modulation. In high-energy film music, it is common to modulate frequently. In low-energy music, modulations are less frequent and may not occur at all.

Of course, modulations are uncommon in some musical styles. While modulations are commonplace in classical music and orchestral film music, they occur less frequently in rock 'n' roll and popular musical styles. If the stylistic choice for the project is a style that doesn't employ modulations, then modulations are uncommon regardless of the energy level of the music.

An example of a low-energy musical cue is "A Tree for My Bed" from *Jurassic Park* (Universal Studios, 1993). Composed by John Williams, the cue begins as a soft celesta solo. As the music proceeds, the instrumentation expands slightly, adding in woodwinds, harp, and strings. Large instrumentation structures, such as loud brass and percussion, are avoided entirely. At the end of the cue, the instrumentation returns to a soft celesta solo. The tempo is very slow, approximately 46 beats per minute. Most of the music uses two subdivisions per beat. The music does not modulate, remaining in D major throughout. The harmonic rhythm varies. At times, there is one chord per measure and occasionally two or three. In all, "A Tree for My Bed" uses musical structures common in low-energy cues, particularly small instrumentation, slow tempos, and infrequent modulations.

An example of a high-energy musical cue is "The Sea Monster" from *Sinbad: Legend of the Seven Seas* (DreamWorks, 2003). Composed by Harry Gregson-Williams, the cue uses extremely large instrumentation. All instruments in a traditional orchestra are employed, including woodwinds, brass, percussion, and strings. "The Sea Monster" uses a fast tempo, approximately 164 beats per minute.

The beat is frequently divided into 4 subdivisions, creating up to 656 subdivisions per minute. Modulations occur frequently, placing each musical phrase in a different key. The harmonic rhythm varies. At times, a single chord will last more than a measure, other times only two beats. In all, "The Sea Monster" uses musical structures common in high-energy cues, particularly large instrumentation, fast tempos, frequent subdivisions of the beat, and frequent modulations.

"Analyzing Musical Energy" is provided in the appendix for analyzing the energy level of a piece of music. Each question addresses a characteristic that impacts musical energy, after which an assessment of the overall energy can be made. As one example, figure 5.1 completes the "Analyzing Musical Energy" worksheet for *Adagio for Strings* by Samuel Barber.

ANALYZING MUSICAL ENERGY

1. What is the tempo?

(1)	2	3	4	5
slow		moderate		fast
(60 bpm or less)				(160 bpm or more)

2. What is the rhythmic subdivision of the beat?

(1)	2	3	4	5
quarter note or less		eighth note		sixteenth note
(≤1 subdivision)		(2 subdivisions)		(≥4 subdivisions)

3. How large is the instrumentation?

1	2	(3)	4	5
small		medium		large

4. How frequently do the chords change (harmonic rhythm)?

1	(2)	3	4	5
rarely	occasionally (every measure)			frequently (every beat)

5. How frequently does the key change (modulations)?

1	(2)	3	4	5
never		occasionally		frequently (every couple of measures)

6. The overall musical energy is:

1	(2)	3	4	5
low		medium		high

FIG. 5.1. Analyzing Musical Energy in *Adagio for Strings*

Adagio for Strings uses a slow tempo and rhythmic subdivision. The instrumentation is string orchestra, smaller than a full orchestra but larger than chamber music. The harmonic rhythm is slow. The music modulates occasionally, beginning in B♭ minor and touching on several related keys before ending back in B♭ minor. Overall, the music produces a low energy level, either 1 or 2 on a scale of 1 to 5.

COORDINATING VISUAL AND MUSICAL ENERGY

Most commonly, the musical energy level is designed to match the visual energy level. Low-energy music is created to match low-energy visuals, and high-energy music is created to enhance high-energy visuals. This is the approach taken in each of the examples discussed so far.

For the opening scene of *The Green Mile*, Thomas Newman composed low-energy music to match the low-energy visuals. The music has almost no discernable tempo, using long notes that gradually fade between various synthesizer and string textures. Occasionally, a few isolated notes are added in piano and low register percussion, all treated with a large amount of reverb. The result is a floating musical texture that matches the low energy of the visuals.

The low-energy cue "A Tree for My Bed" was composed to accompany a low-energy scene in *Jurassic Park*. As night falls, Dr. Grant takes shelter in a large tree with the children, Lex and Tim. They talk quietly before drifting off to sleep. The scene has little visual activity, as the characters are sitting without moving. The scene does not include any picture cuts, using a single shot that slowly zooms out.

For the high-energy opening scene of *Revenge of the Sith*, John Williams composed music that is rhythmically active, using fast tempos and multiple subdivisions of each beat. The music is also very large in instrumentation, using full orchestra with frequent melodic statements by the brass section. The music also shifts and evolves frequently, changing keys, instrumentation, and tempo. All of these characteristics create high-energy music that enhances the high-energy visuals.

The high-energy cue "The Sea Monster" was composed to accompany a high-energy fight pitting Sinbad against a giant sea monster. Sailors jump around, swing swords, light explosives, and throw ropes. The sea monster flails about, attacking the sailors and their ship with large tentacles. To win the fight, Sinbad and his childhood friend Prince Proteus cut free two of the ship's largest beams and use them to spear the sea monster. The scene uses over one hundred picture cuts during a three-minute battle. The scene includes moving camera effects, such as when the camera follows the sea monster's tentacles through the air.

Notably, when music is synced to visual images, the creative team has additional tools to increase the energy level of a scene. Most significantly, aligning shifts in the structure of the music with picture cuts will raise the energy level. The shift in the music can be a myriad of techniques—an increase in instrumentation, a change in the harmony, a new meter, a new melody, a shift in the melodic instrumentation, and so on. In both the opening scene of *Revenge of the Sith* and "The Sea Monster," significant changes in the music are aligned with picture cuts to further raise the energy level of the scene.

In the vast majority of cases, the music matches the energy level of the visuals. Nonetheless, that is not the only option for the creative team. For a moment, let's imagine a high-energy battle scene. Commonly, the music selected for such a scene is high-energy action music. That was the choice for the opening scene of *Revenge of the Sith* and "The Sea Monster." However, a creative team should feel free to make a different choice if they feel it is appropriate, including using slow sustained music or no music at all. Typically, this choice is made when the desired emotional outcome supersedes the visual energy level, such as a scene that conveys the sadness of war by combining slow music with high-energy battle footage.

Troy retells the story of the *Iliad* by Homer. The city of Troy is besieged by a coalition of Greek armies. After several setbacks in battle, the Greek armies build a large wooden horse and hide a handful of soldiers within. The people of Troy, believing the horse to be a gift for the gods, bring the horse into the city. At night, the hidden soldiers exit the horse and open the city gates, allowing the full Greek army to pour in. In the score, when the Greek soldiers charge through the city gates, James Horner composed slow and sustained music. For the first minute of the battle, a single note is sustained in low register strings while a lyrical vocal line is sung on top. In this case, the slow music enhances the tragedy and sadness of the fall of Troy. After a minute of slow music, the score shifts to large action music that matches the high energy of the battle.

The beginning of *Saving Private Ryan* (DreamWorks, 1998) depicts the invasion of Omaha Beach on June 6, 1944. The scene includes all the visual characteristics of a high-energy scene—a great deal of movement by people and objects on-screen, frequent picture cuts, and moving camera effects. Nonetheless, the scene uses no music at all. In this case, the lack of music magnifies the realism of the historical events. The absence of music also gives the sound effects a more prominent role in the scene, allowing the explosions and gunfire to drive the energy of the scene.

DISCUSSION AND DECISION-MAKING

During discussion and analysis, it can be helpful to express energy level as a number on a scale of 1 to 5. A rating of 1 is low-energy, 3 is medium-energy, and 5 is high-energy. A conversation between two sitting characters with infrequent picture cuts and a stationary camera is a low-energy scene, expressed as 1 on the scale. A scene where soldiers prepare for battle with occasional picture cuts and a stationary camera is a medium-energy scene, expressed as 3 on the scale. An intense battle scene with frequent picture cuts and moving camera effects is a high-energy scene, expressed as 5 on the scale. Expressing energy level as a number helps each creative team member solidify their opinion and communicate that opinion to other team members. In addition, over time, specific creative ideas become associated with each number on the scale, facilitating the creative process in music selection and composition.

In filmmaking, the picture is made before the music. As such, the first step for the creative team is to analyze the energy level of the picture. Next, the creative team must decide: should the energy level of the music match the energy level of the visuals? In the vast majority of cases, the answer is yes. However, the creative team can choose to align low-energy music with high-energy visuals, or vice versa. Ultimately, the creative team must analyze the energy level of the visuals, decide whether to match that energy level with the music, and then create music that realizes this vision.

CHAPTER 6

Dialogue and Sound Effects

Films have a variety of sounds in addition to music, including dialogue and sound effects. To avoid creating a cluttered audio landscape, the music must complement the other audio elements.

By its strictest definition, the term "dialogue" refers to a conversation between two or more characters. Of course, there are additional types of speech in a film. A "voiceover" is commentary stated by an off-screen narrator. A "monologue" is a speech given by a single character. While each term defines a specific type of speech, the term "dialogue" is commonly used in casual conversation to refer collectively to all types of speech in a film. For our purposes, we will use the term "dialogue" by its collective definition, meaning any type of speech in a film.

Sound effects are sounds that are directly associated with objects and events on screen. A barking dog, a punch in the face, a ringing doorbell, and a shooting gun are all visual events that would have corresponding sound effects. In each case, the audience perceives a visual element as the source of the sound. Notably, ambient speech—such as crowd noise and restaurant chatter—is best treated as a sound effect. In this case, the audience is not expected to listen to or understand each individual word. The sounds are ambient noises linked to the setting of the scene, comparable to birds chirping in a field.

When multiple audio elements exist simultaneously, only one element can be featured as the foreground material. The foreground element captures the primary attention of the audience. It is the element the audience focuses on and thinks about. Background elements are plainly audible but are not the primary focus of the audience. The audience hears and is aware of background elements but prioritizes the foreground elements in their mind.

When dialogue or sound effects are foreground material, the music must recede to the background. When dialogue and sound effects relinquish the foreground, the music can be featured as the foreground.

ACCOMMODATING DIALOGUE

When dialogue is present, it is the foreground material. All types of dialogue deliver vital information about the story. Dialogue also changes continuously, so the audience must listen closely to every word to understand its meaning. As such, dialogue always demands the audience's primary focus and attention. When music is present at the same time as dialogue, the music must be positioned in the background to respect the foreground role of dialogue.

There are a variety of compositional techniques that move music behind dialogue. These compositional techniques include small instrumentation, sustained textures, soft tone colors, a condensed pitch range, repetition, no melody, no vocals, and no music at all.

Music that uses small instrumentation naturally recedes to the background. This technique is extremely common and employed at some point in nearly every film. One example is the cue "Remembering Petticoat Lane" from *Jurassic Park*. In the scene, John Hammond and Dr. Sattler have a conversation while sitting at a buffet table. Mr. Hammond recalls the first amusement park he ever built and explains how he hoped Jurassic Park would be different. John Williams scored the scene with small instrumentation, beginning with just celesta and harp. As the scene proceeds, soft strings and a solo horn lightly supplement the musical texture. The music avoids large portions of the orchestra, using no percussion, woodwinds, or forceful brass instruments such as trumpets. In this case, the small instrumentation ensures the audience's focus remains on the dialogue.

Sustained textures that lack rhythmic activity naturally recede to the background. One example occurs near the beginning of *Inception* (Warner Brothers, 2010). At the beginning of the film, the main character Cobb washes ashore a beach. He is captured by men with guns and taken to a private meeting with the character Saito. The guards seat Cobb at the table and place his belongings—a gun and a spinning top—in front of Saito. Saito then speaks. Saito asks Cobb why he is there and whether he plans to kill him. Saito then picks up the spinning top and recalls a man he once met, long ago, who had the same toy. During the conversation, Hans Zimmer composed a sustained texture that combines tremolo strings and synthesizers. A long note in tremolo strings swells up and down. As the tremolo fades out, a long note swells up in low register synthesizers. The overall texture lacks any perceptible beat that the listener could tap along to. In this case, the sustained nature of the music ensures that the music remains subordinate to the dialogue.

A focus on instruments with soft tone colors can help music recede to the background. Some instruments have piercing and forceful tone colors, such as trumpets, crash cymbals, and distorted guitar. These instruments demand the listener's attention and directly compete for the foreground. By contrast, some instruments have soft and gentle tone colors. Sustained strings, low register flute, ambient synthesizers—these instruments are placid and smooth. They naturally fade to the background in the presence of dialogue. One example occurs in the cue "Journey to the Island" from *Jurassic Park*. In the scene, the main characters fly in a helicopter to an island amusement park populated by living dinosaurs. At the beginning of the scene, the point of view is located outside of the helicopter and the audience sees the helicopter flying over the ocean. At this point, there is no dialogue in the scene, allowing John Williams to compose a large orchestral theme. The melody is placed in forte trumpets, and the beginning of the phrase is accented with a cymbal crash. As the scene progresses, a picture cut moves the point of view inside the helicopter and dialogue begins. John Hammond, the businessman and park designer, talks about the strong winds on the island and how the helicopter ride can be a bit bumpy. The other passengers attempt to put on their seatbelts while Mr. Hammond gives them instructions. During the dialogue, John Williams shifted the music to softer tone colors. Rather than continuing with the melody in trumpets, the melody moves to sustained strings and woodwinds. During the dialogue, cymbals crashes are avoided entirely. After a period of dialogue, a picture cut returns the point of view to the outside of the helicopter. The audience now views images of the helicopter flying along the island's ridges and waterfalls. At this point, the dialogue stops and the music returns to the foreground. The music revisits the trumpet melodic statement and cymbal crashes. In this case, John Williams used the softer tone colors of woodwinds and strings to place the music in the background when dialogue entered the scene. When the dialogue stopped, Williams moved the music to the foreground with the more forceful tone colors of forte trumpets and cymbal crashes.

Using a condensed pitch range can help music recede to the background. Musical instruments span a wide pitch range from low to high. Large instruments (e.g., bass, tuba, contrabassoon) produce pitches in the low register. Small instruments (e.g., violin, piccolo) produce pitches in the upper register. Music that utilizes this full range, including the low, middle, and upper registers, feels large and expansive. Music that focuses on only one register feels small and contained, which can situate the music in the background. One example occurs in *Back to the Future*. In the 81st minute of the film, George McFly sees two people tussling in a car outside his high school dance. He opens the door and finds Biff, the school bully, manhandling Lorraine Baines. They have a conversation, during which Elaine asks for help, Biff threatens George, and George tells Biff to leave. For the music, Alan Silvestri scored the conversation with upper register violins. No instruments in the low or middle registers are used. In this case, limiting the music to the extreme upper register ensures the music remains in the background. At the end of the conversation, George saves the day by punching out Biff.

Musical ideas that are predictable and repetitive naturally fade to the background. This phenomenon is not limited to music. Any sound that is repetitive and predictable fades to the background, while sounds that change and surprise grab a listener's attention. For instance, a traditional analog clock makes a repetitive clicking sound. The second hand moves once per second, and an audible click accompanies the motion. Listeners immediately sense the pattern, after which they pay little or no attention to the sound. Now, imagine the clock is located in a dining room during a family gathering. Everyone in the room is talking and telling stories. The conversation is unpredictable and constantly changing. Every word provides each listener with new information. Meanwhile, the clock sound continues as a repetitive click-click-click. In this situation, listeners naturally focus their attention on the unpredictable conversation, while the predictable clock sound fades to the background.

Film music can take advantage of this phenomenon and use repetition to keep music subordinate to dialogue. One example occurs in the opening scene of *The Truman Show* (Paramount Pictures, 1998). In the scene, various characters are interviewed on-screen about the authenticity of *The Truman Show*. In between each interview, Truman is shown talking to himself in a bathroom mirror. Overall, the first two minutes of the film are dominated by dialogue. For the scene, Burkhard Dallwitz composed a cue that uses rhythmic repetition to stay behind the dialogue. The cue uses a steady eighth note pattern in pulsing synthesizers. Once established, the pulse does not change during the entire cue. In addition, predictable rhythmic patterns are used in the melody and harmony. The melody is a series of short phrases in upper register piano. Each phrase is a series of eighth notes that begins as a pickup to beat 3 of the measure. While the melody emphasizes beat 3, the harmony emphasizes beat 1. Low register piano plays a short arpeggio on the downbeat. Electric bass changes pitch only on downbeats. Sustained strings and synthesizers change chords only on downbeats. All of these elements establish a rhythmic pattern and do not vary from the pattern. Notably, the cue does contain a few musical surprises. At several points, tambourine and low-register drums come in suddenly. Since these elements are unexpected, they demand a great deal of attention from the listener. To ensure that they don't pull attention away from the dialogue, the percussion hits are only used in pauses in between the dialogue. In summary, the musical elements that are repetitive and predictable are used during dialogue, while the musical elements that are surprising and unexpected are placed in the pauses in between the dialogue.

Music that removes or minimizes the melody naturally fades behind dialogue. Melody, essentially by definition, grabs a listener's attention. Melody is the foreground part of the music—the element a listener is most likely to sing along to. As a result, melody can pull a listener's attention away from dialogue. By contrast, removing melody can ensure that music recedes to the background. One example is the main title sequence of *Antz* (DreamWorks, 1998). *Antz* tells the story of an individualistic worker ant who falls in love with a princess and saves his colony from an evil military commander. At the 2-minute mark of the film, a sequence of visual images introduces the audience to the ant colony. Expansive shots show tall pillars of dirt and thousands of worker ants moving rocks. During these images, Harry Gregson-Williams and John Powell scored a prominent melodic statement. The melody is stated twice, first as an eight-bar phrase with the melody in a whistling sound and second as an eight-bar phrase with the melody in violins. During these two phrases, the melody demands a great deal of attention and dominates the audience's experience. Next, the picture shifts and dialogue begins. An official ant sorts baby ant larvae into future workers and soldiers. A group of ants completes an exercise routine while a lead ant gives instructions. During these scenes with dialogue, the music shifts to a groove-based structure dominated by rhythmic drums. For much of this section, there is no melody at all. When melody does enter, it's a short motive lasting only a few beats. Each small melodic motive is placed in pauses between lines of dialogue. Next, the dialogue ends and the visuals return to expansive images of the full colony carrying rocks and dirt. Once the dialogue has stopped, the music returns to a large melodic statement. The melody is presented in trumpets and violins as a full eight-bar phrase. In this opening sequence of *Antz*, prominent melodic statements are made only in the absence of dialogue. When dialogue is present, the melody is minimized or entirely removed.

Music that employs tone colors similar to the foreground material can interfere with the foreground. In the case of dialogue, music that includes singing and other forms of vocals has a similar tone color to the foreground material. In most projects, the score music is exclusively instrumental, which ensures there are not vocal elements interfering with dialogue. In other cases, vocals are employed, but the vocals do not use a recognizable language. Generic "ooo" and "ahh" vocals function much like non-vocal instrumentals; they avoid discernable language that could interfere with the dialogue. Still other projects will use Latin or a made-up primitive language, while the foreground dialogue is in present-day English. Of course, some projects do use vocals in the music, particularly projects that wish to appeal to a young demographic by incorporating contemporary songs. In these cases, the creative team must be aware that the vocals could interfere with dialogue and seek additional methods to keep the music in the background.

Last but not least, removing the music entirely ensures that dialogue remains in the foreground. This is a simple but important technique, and it is used extensively in nearly every film. One example occurs at the beginning of *Air Force One* (Columbia Pictures, 1997). The film opens with a long main title sequence that presents the name of the film, production company, and actors. During the main title, Jerry Goldsmith composed a large and sweeping orchestral theme. Next, a dramatic scene occurs during which soldiers parachute atop a fortified residence, kill the guards, and kidnap a man sleeping within. During this scene, the score uses suspense and action music. Next, the setting shifts to a banquet hall in Russia, where a diplomat introduces the president of the United States. The president proceeds to give a speech. During the speech, the music stops entirely. After the speech, the setting shifts to Air Force One and the dialogue stops. Here, the music reenters and presents a heroic orchestral theme. In this example, the first nine minutes of the film use a great deal of music. The music only stops during the president's speech. Stopping the music entirely ensures that the dialogue receives the full attention of the audience.

In total, we have identified eight compositional techniques that allow music to effectively accompany dialogue. These techniques are often combined and used simultaneously. As previously discussed, the opening scene of *Inception* uses sustained textures to help the music stay behind dialogue. In addition, the cue employs small instrumentation, using tremolo strings and synthesizers while omitting large brass and percussion. The cue utilizes predictability, repeatedly alternating between the tremolo strings and low register synthesizers. The cue also has no melody. In this case, a multitude of compositional techniques ensure the music remains subordinate to the dialogue.

When these compositional techniques are not employed, the only recourse is for the film's mixer to lower the overall volume of the music. In this case, the music is often placed so low in the mix that it makes little or no contribution to the film. By contrast, when the compositional structure of the music places it in the background, the music can be placed at a louder volume in the overall mix. It is always best if the compositional characteristics of the music ensure the music remains subordinate to dialogue.

ALTERNATING DIALOGUE AND MUSIC

Scenes with dialogue present the creative team with a twofold choice. The first option is to create a compositional structure that accommodates dialogue and maintains that structure for the entire scene. The previously discussed example "Petticoat Lane" takes this approach. John Williams scored the scene with small instrumentation and never increased to large instrumentation. In this case, the small instrumentation technique is employed for the entire scene and the music remains in the background throughout.

The second option is to pass the listener's attention between dialogue and music. When dialogue is present, the music is small and in the background. When dialogue pauses, the music expands and moves to the foreground. The previously discussed example "Journey to the Island" takes this approach. Also scored by John Williams, the scene began with no dialogue and a foreground musical statement. When the dialogue started, the music used softer tone colors and smaller instrumentation to recede to the background. When the dialogue subsequently stopped, the music expanded and shifted back to the foreground. In this case, the foreground element alternates between dialogue and music.

Of these two approaches, which is best for a given scene is a subjective choice to be made by the creative team. Commonly, the first approach is preferred in scenes with minimal breaks in the dialogue. By contrast, the second approach is best when there is no dialogue for notable portions of the scene. Perhaps dialogue begins ten seconds into the scene, allowing the music to make a foreground statement at the beginning of the scene. Perhaps the dialogue pauses in the middle of the scene, allowing the music to temporarily move to the foreground. Long pauses can be filled with a full melodic phrase, and short pauses can be filled by percussion hits.

Regardless of the ultimate choice, these possibilities mean the creative team should always closely analyze the timing of dialogue in a scene. When does the dialogue start? When does the dialogue stop? Are the pauses in the dialogue, moments the music can temporarily expand? These questions should always be asked or else opportunities to make a foreground musical statement will be overlooked.

HIGH-ENERGY SCENES WITH DIALOGUE

High-energy scenes with dialogue present a specific challenge for the creative team. High-energy visuals demand large music that helps drive the energy of the scene. Simultaneously, the presence of dialogue demands small music that accommodates the foreground role of the dialogue.

A creative team presented with this challenge has two options. First, music can be created that has two structural levels, such as large instrumentation and medium instrumentation. The large instrumentation is used in pauses in the dialogue, and the medium instrumentation is used during dialogue. This approach was used in "The Sea Monster" from *Sinbad: Legend of the Seven Seas*. During the scene, Sinbad and Prince Proteus talk to one another as they battle the sea monster. As is often the case in such scenes, the dialogue is sporadic. A character will deliver a line, then go back to battling the monster. Musically, the largest moments occur in the spaces in the dialogue. These moments use full orchestra, trumpet melodic statements, fast tempos, and a quick rhythmic subdivision. During dialogue, the music shifts to smaller instrumentation, focusing on strings, woodwinds, and horns while omitting the large trumpet melodies. A fast tempo and quick rhythmic subdivision are maintained, ensuring that the music continues to match the high energy of the visuals.

The second option for high-energy scenes with dialogue is to strategically use predictability. Large instrumentation and fast rhythms can fade to the background if they use a repetitive rhythmic pattern and consistent instrumentation. One example that employs this technique occurs in *Inception*. At the 9-minute mark of the film, Cobb, Arthur, Mal, and Saito are having a tense conversation when gunfire erupts. The ensuing visuals are extremely high-energy, including gunfire, dashing characters, and collapsing buildings. Amidst the chaos, the dialogue continues as characters occasionally shout to one another. Musically, Hans Zimmer composed a large instrumentation cue using guitar, synthesizers, rhythmic strings, and full brass. The music is rhythmically active throughout, using a fast tempo and quick rhythmic subdivision. When dialogue enters, the large instrumentation and quick rhythms are not altered. Despite this, the music sits well in the mix and does not interfere with the dialogue because of the use of repetition. Each instrument establishes a rhythmic pattern and subsequently repeats it for the full cue. Beginning with the initial gunfire, the violins establish an eighth-note pattern in the upper register. The low brass perform a long diminuendo, one chord every six beats. The horns establish a countermelody, one note every three beats. Each of these elements, once established, continues unaltered throughout the cue. In this case, predictability in the rhythmic structure of the music allows the large instrumentation to continue even in the presence of dialogue.

SOUND EFFECTS

Sound effects present a different challenge for the creative team. In some cases, sound effects are foreground material and the music must recede to the background. In other cases, sound effects are background material and the music can take the foreground space. Given these different scenarios, the first step of the decision-making process is to determine whether the sound effects play a foreground or background role.

When sound effects are foreground material, they capture the primary attention of the audience. The audience becomes keenly aware of and thinks specifically about the sound effects. Typically, this is the case when the sound effects are unexpected, provide new information to the audience, or are associated with the main idea in the plot. When at least one of these criteria is met, the sound effects advance to the foreground.

One notable scenario is when a plot development occurs off screen and the audience is only aware of it because of the sound effects. The film *Charade* (Universal Pictures, 1963) uses this technique during the 13th minute of the film. Regina Lampert returns home to her apartment in Paris. While the audience is shown an image of Regina standing in her apartment, they hear the sound of a doorknob being turned. Next, the creak of a door being opened. Then, the sound of footsteps. At this moment, the sound effects are the primary plot device. Someone has entered Regina's apartment, and the only way the audience has this information is to hear the sound effects. In this case, the sound effects are the foreground material, and all other audio must stay in the background. The dialogue stops entirely at this point. The score, composed by Henry Mancini, uses sustained strings and soft piano. The small instrumentation and sustained textures ensure the music remains in the background. By placing the dialogue and music in the background, they avoid conflicting with the foreground sound effects.

In other cases, the main idea of the plot is shown directly on screen and the main idea is something that requires sound effects. In *Back to the Future*, Dr. Emmett Brown builds a nuclear powered time machine. To acquire fuel, he steals plutonium from terrorists. In the 28th minute of the film, Dr. Brown plans his first attempt at time travel in a shopping mall parking lot. Unfortunately, the terrorists show up to exact revenge. They speed into the parking lot and begin shooting at Dr. Brown. At this moment, the arrival of the terrorists is the main idea in the plot. The sound of the gunfire is directly associated with the main idea and therefore draws a great deal of attention from the audience. Accordingly, the dialogue and music must recede behind the sound effects. In this case, the dialogue pauses each time gunfire erupts. The music, scored by Alan Silvestri, is characterized by repetition, which makes it stay in the background. Over a minute before the terrorists arrive, Silvestri establishes a rhythmic groove in percussion and strings. The rhythmic pattern repeats for almost two minutes. In this case, the music is predictable and repetitive, pushing it to the background. Meanwhile, the gunfire is unexpected and surprising, advancing it to the foreground.

When music must recede behind sound effects, the music can feature the same techniques noted with dialogue. Small instrumentation, sustained textures, soft tone colors, a condensed pitch range, repetition, no melody, avoiding tone colors similar to the foreground material, and no music at all will ensure that the music stays behind foreground sound effects. In the case of sound effects, tone colors that are similar to the foreground material are traditional instruments rather than vocals. For instance, drums have a tone color similar to gunfire. It is a common approach to remove percussion in the presence of gunfire and explosion sound effects.

In many cases, the sound effects are background material. The sound effects are not the primary focus of the audience, and the foreground space can be taken by either the music or dialogue. One example is the opening scene of *Pulp Fiction* (Miramax, 1994). The characters Pumpkin and Honey Bunny dine at a café while planning their next robbery. The scene has a variety of background sound effects, including the sound of clinking dishware, passing traffic, and background conversation. The music is a barely audible lounge piano cue, placed low in the mix as source music. Notably, music used in this manner is very similar to sound effects. The music is ambient sound associated with the plot location, just like the sound of clinking dishware. In this case, the main idea of the scene is the conversation between Pumpkin and Honey Bunny. The music and sound effects are background material associated with the scene's café location.

In the *Pulp Fiction* scene, the background sound effects allow the dialogue to advance to the foreground. In other cases, placing the sound effects in the background allows the music to advance to the foreground. One instance occurs in the film *Hook* (TriStar Pictures, 1991). At the beginning of *Hook*, Peter Pan is living as an adult corporate lawyer in San Francisco. He has lost the memories of his previous life as Peter Pan. During the film, he returns to Neverland to rescue his children, who have been kidnapped by Captain Hook. In the 100th minute of the film, Peter Pan rediscovers his ability to fly. He leaps into the air and soars high above Neverland. At this moment, John Williams states the main theme of the film using full orchestra. During the soaring melodic statements, the sound effects are reduced to a barely audible rustling of wind. In addition, the dialogue pauses at this point. At this moment, the dialogue and sound effects fade to the background as the music advances to the foreground.

DECISION-MAKING

When making decisions about the music, the creative team must first determine if the music will be foreground or background material. For analysis, decision-makers can consider a series of questions. Is there dialogue? When dialogue is present, it is the foreground material. If there is dialogue, is there anywhere the dialogue pauses or stops? Often, the music can move to the foreground when there are breaks in the dialogue. Are there sound effects? If so, are the sound effects foreground or background material? If there are foreground sound effects, the music must remain in the background. If there are background sound effects and no dialogue, then the music can advance to the foreground.

When the music must be background material, decision-makers must devise the best way to achieve this objective. Any one or a combination of the compositional techniques discussed in this chapter can be used to achieve this goal. To facilitate the process of working with dialogue and sound effects, "Dialogue and Sound Effects" is provided in the appendix.

CHAPTER 7

Contour

Film is an art form that evolves over time. It is not a single picture or static image, but rather a moving image and an unfolding story. Exactly how and when the story changes can be called "contour."

Likewise, music is an art form that manifests over time. Music does not exist in a single instance, but rather as a series of notes, chords, and melodies that unfold gradually.

The creative team must decide if and how to synchronize the contour of the film with the contour of the music. In some cases, changes in the music will align precisely with changes in the picture. In other cases, the picture will change while the music maintains a constant musical structure. In this chapter, we will look at considerations when making these choices.

CONTOUR OF THE PICTURE

Shifts in the contour of the picture are driven by changes in the story that give the audience new information. The new information results in the audience feeling a new emotion, experiencing a new energy level, or pondering a new plot circumstance.

For instance, suppose a man and woman are talking casually at the end of a date. At first, they are talking about trivial events amongst their friends. Then the man gets down on one knee and says, "I've always loved you. Will you marry me?" The woman nods affirmatively, and they kiss.

In such a scene, the man's proposal is a shift in the story. Prior to the proposal, the audience had no idea if the man would ever have the courage to tell the woman how he feels. The audience likely hoped the couple would get together but did not view the casual conversation as particularly significant. At the proposal, the audience's thoughts and feelings shift. The audience realizes this is an important moment—the climactic proposal after a long courtship. The audience would experience an increase in excitement and anticipation. Likewise, the moment they kiss represents another shift in the story. The woman has reciprocated the man's feelings, and the couple has gotten together. Accordingly, the audience's feelings would shift from hope and anticipation to satisfaction and resolution.

Changes in energy level are also shifts in contour. Suppose the bad guys are chasing the hero through crowded streets. The picture uses typical high-energy techniques, including frequent picture cuts and quick movement of objects and characters. Suddenly, the hero ducks into a dark alleyway and hides. At this moment, the picture shifts from high energy to low energy. In this case, the new information for the audience is a drop in energy level: the hero is hiding rather than running.

Shifts in contour are commonly facilitated by a picture cut or change in dialogue. A picture cut is a sudden change in the audience's vantage point. Picture cuts can be used to show a new location, a new character, or a different perspective of a given scene. As a result, picture cuts often provide new information to the audience and produce a shift in contour. In regards to dialogue, the entrance or exit of dialogue may facilitate a shift in contour. Likewise, the most important line in a scene, such as a key joke or proposal, is often a shift in contour.

While the specific details of contour shifts vary greatly from scene to scene, the key ingredient is a change in the audience's experience. Any event that provides the audience with new information, creating a change in the audience's experience, is a shift in contour.

CREATING HITS

A "hit" is a change in the music synchronized with a change in the picture. Hits are also called "synchronization points" or "sync points." The most stereotypical example of a hit is a cymbal crash synchronized with a picture cut. Of course, there are many additional ways music can hit a change in the picture.

In our hypothetical story about the proposal followed by a kiss, the creative team may decide to hit the kiss. Perhaps the instrumentation increases to full orchestra, the harmony resolves to tonic, the dynamics increase to forte, the melody moves to violins, and a new theme is presented. In such an instance, the creative team has aligned multiple changes in the music with a change in the story.

Once the creative team has decided to hit a given event, it must next decide precisely how to hit it. "Characteristics of Change in Music" in the appendix includes a list of musical characteristics that can change when there is a change in the picture. The list can function as a starting point for a creative team deciding how best to hit a given visual event. Let's elaborate on each possibility.

Increase or Decrease Overall Instrumentation. It is common to increase instrumentation to match higher energy visuals or to move the music to the foreground. Conversely, it is common to decrease instrumentation to match lower energy visuals or to move the music behind dialogue. Increasing instrumentation is the most noticeable way to create a hit. Creative teams who value directness will commonly increase instrumentation at hit points, while those who prefer subtlety are more likely to decrease instrumentation or use other methods.

Change Foreground Tone Color. It is common to move the melody from one instrument to another at a hit point, which creates a shift in the tone color of the music. Notably, the music does not need to use a traditional melody to employ this effect. The foreground musical idea can be a general musical texture that changes tone color at the hit point.

Change Scale Type. Scale type has a significant affect on the emotional impact of the music. Accordingly, a change from one scale to another is particularly useful when the hit point initiates a shift in emotion. Of course, it is possible to change the scale type without changing tonic, such as a shift from D major to D minor.

Move Tonic. Changing the pitch that is heard as tonic creates a noticeable shift in the music. Accordingly, moving the listener's perception of tonic is one of the most common types of hits. It is possible to change tonic with or without changing the scale type. A modulation from C major to F major moves tonic without changing scale type. A modulation from C major to E minor changes both tonic and scale type.

Increase/Decrease Dissonance Level. The dissonance level and the types of chords have a significant affect on the emotional impact of the music. Dissonance can be increased when the hit point makes the story scarier or more upsetting. Dissonance is typically decreased when tensions are resolved.

Increase/Decrease Harmonic Rhythm. Harmonic rhythm is how frequently the chords change in a progression. Typically, harmonic rhythm is increased when the creative team wishes to increase energy in the music.

Arrive at Significant Harmonies. It is common to place a significant harmonic arrival at a hit point. Perhaps the music resolves to tonic or arrives on dominant. Or perhaps the music has been on tonic before the hit and then shifts away from it at the hit.

Introduce a New Melody or Musical Idea. When a hit point introduces a character or starts a new section, it is common to use the hit to begin a new melody or musical idea.

Restate a Previous Theme. Most films reuse musical ideas throughout the project. When a hit point revisits a recurring character, emotion, or plot situation, it is common to restate a previous theme.

End a Melody or Musical Idea. Just as a hit point can be used to start a new musical idea, it can also be used to end a musical idea. Aligning a cadence or the last note of a musical idea with a hit point can be very effective. This idea is particularly common when the picture cuts to black at the end of a scene.

Change Melodic Phrasing. Most melodies are built with four- and eight-bar phrases. Of course, music can be written with shorter phrases or odd measure groupings. One way to create a hit is to move between sections with different phrasing structures.

Change Meter. Changing meter, such as shifting from 4/4 to 3/4, can be used to create a hit.

Change Rhythmic Emphasis within the Meter. Music can shift rhythmic emphasis without changing meter. Suppose the music is in 4/4 meter and emphasizes every beat. This idea is followed by a new idea, also in 4/4 meter, that places accents on beat 1 and the eighth-note subdivision of beat 2. Changing the placement of accents within a meter can be used to create a hit.

Increase/Decrease Beat Subdivision. A shift in beat subdivision changes the shortest rhythmic unit of the music, such as shifting from an eighth-note to sixteenth-note subdivision. The subdivision is typically shortened when the hit point is an increase in energy level. The subdivision is typically lengthened when the hit point is a decrease in energy level.

Increase/Decrease Tempo. Increasing tempo is common when the hit point initiates a higher energy section. Decreasing tempo is common when the hit point initiates a lower energy section.

Stop/Start the Music. One of the most dramatic ways to hit an event is to stop the music. Particularly for creative teams who value subtlety and nuance, stopping the music when audiences are expecting a big climax can be very appealing. Likewise, musical entrances typically occur at turning points in the plot.

Change the Overall Compositional Structure. Typically, musical passages can be described in terms of an overall compositional structure, such as melody plus harmonic accompaniment, four-part counterpoint, or a homophonic chord progression. Shifting from one compositional structure to another at a hit point can create a subtle but significant shift.

Change the Overall Pitch Register. Music can emphasize the low register, mid register, or upper register. Or music can span the full range from low to upper register. Changing the pitch register of the music can create an effective hit.

Change Dynamic Markings. Any instrument can be played with a range of dynamics from soft to loud. A shift in the dynamic markings from soft to loud, or vice versa, can create an impactful shift in the music.

Change Performance Techniques. Specific performance techniques such as trills and glissandi can create a specific mood or texture. Starting or ending a specific performance technique at a hit point can be a contour shift in the music.

Change Recording Techniques. Specific recording techniques such as EQ and delays can create a specific mood or texture. Starting or ending a specific recording technique at a hit point can be a contour shift in the music.

Notably, these techniques are not mutually exclusive, meaning creative teams can employ more than one technique simultaneously. Frequently, the most effective hits combine multiple techniques, such as decreasing instrumentation while moving tonic, lowering dynamic markings, and contracting the overall pitch register—or increasing instrumentation while moving tonic, raising dynamic markings, and expanding the overall pitch register.

TO HIT OR NOT TO HIT

There is a change in the picture. Should there be a corresponding change in the music? Ultimately, there is not one universal answer to this question. In each instance, the creative team has to weigh various factors and then make the choice they believe to be best for the project.

Invariably, a film will contain thousands of picture cuts, some of which will be hit with a change in the music and some of which will not. Picture cuts associated with new information are more frequently hit than picture cuts that do not deliver new information. Suppose the main character is speaking. A picture cut changes the vantage point from the right side of the character's face to the left side of their face. In this case, the picture cut delivers little new information and likely does not warrant a change in the music. On the other hand, suppose the picture cut reveals a villain sneaking up on the main character. Now, the picture cut delivers new information and a change in the plot. In this case, a shift to more ominous music is likely warranted. When deciding whether to hit a picture cut, the creative team can ask the question—does the picture cut deliver new information to the audience?

An additional consideration is the overall energy level of the scene. Frequent hits are one method for raising the overall energy level. During a high-energy car chase, the creative team may choose to hit a multitude of picture cuts. By contrast, in a low-energy scene where a single character casually walks around a field, the creative team may choose to hit no picture cuts at all.

The overall style of the project can factor in how many events are hit. In some styles, it is customary to hit as many events as possible. In particular, animation and comedies typically hit more visual events than other styles do.

One reason to avoid a specific hit is to increase musical coherence. Perhaps the creative team wishes to present a musical theme as a logical, connected sixteen-bar phrase. Placing a shift in the middle of the phrase would make the music more fragmented. When the primary goal of the creative team is to present a musical theme, it can be desirable to ignore a picture cut or two in order to create a coherent musical phrase.

One last factor is the personal taste of the creative team. Some creative professionals simply prefer to hit fewer events than others. In some cases, musical hits are deemed distracting. When a change in the music aligns with a change in the picture, the audience's attention can shift to the music. For a creative professional who prefers the music to remain in the background, musical hits can be deemed undesirable. In addition, professionals who are accustomed to licensing pre-existing music often grow to prefer fewer hits. Pre-existing music is not written to picture. As such, it is difficult to get the music to follow every twist and turn in the plot and hit every picture cut. More commonly, the music will generally convey the emotions of a scene for thirty seconds or so, and then change to a new piece of music. While this can be an effective method for scoring a project, the music typically hits fewer events than a custom score created by a composer.

Professionals who typically license music can grow accustomed to how such a score feels and subsequently prefer to hit less even after hiring a composer. By contrast, professionals who are used to working with a composer typically prefer to hit more events.

In the end, a creative team must weigh these various factors in each situation and come to a decision as to whether to hit a given visual event.

SPOTTING

Spotting is the process of deciding when to start and stop the music in a film. In many projects, the creative team will hold a formal spotting session, which is a meeting between the director, composer, music editor, and other creative team members. During the spotting session, the team will discuss when music should start and stop in a film.

As noted, starting or stopping the music is one way to hit a visual event. Like other contour decisions, starting and stopping the music typically occurs at turning points in the plot. An event will occur that changes the audience's experience, and the music will start or stop to enhance the plot change. There are several additional situations that often facilitate a start or stop in the music.

The entrance or exit of dialogue. Music often starts when dialogue stops, and vice versa.

To highlight a joke or key line of dialogue. In a scene that includes dialogue from beginning to end, it can be the case that one line of dialogue is more important than all the rest. The creative team can stop the music just before the line as a means of highlighting its importance. While this technique can be used in any genre, it is particularly effective to highlight jokes in comedies. The music can pause before the joke and subsequently resume after the joke as the audience laughs.

To enhance a change in energy. Music often starts when the energy level suddenly increases. For instance, if a character gets up and begins to run, the music may start to enhance the increase in visual energy. Likewise, the music often stops when the energy level dramatically decreases.

When a scene becomes more or less emotional. Music is typically used during the most emotional moments of a film and often exits when the story becomes trivial or lighthearted.

Notably, in nearly all of these cases, starting or stopping the music is not the only plausible solution. Suppose a man and woman are talking over dinner. Suddenly, the woman realizes the man is a double agent seeking to harm her. The woman abruptly stops talking, gets up, and runs.

At such a moment, the dialogue stops and the visual energy increases, creating an opportunity for a hit point. One solution is to have no music during the conversation and begin music at the hit point. Another solution is to use sustained strings during the conversation and then increase tempo, instrumentation, and rhythmic subdivision at the hit point.

From this vantage point, spotting a film is merely the tip of the iceberg in regards to contour decisions. While a spotting session typically identifies the most important contour shifts in a picture, those moments can become starts or stops in the music—or other shifts such as a change in tempo or key. In addition, a spotting session often overlooks subtle shifts in the picture that the creative team will subsequently decide to hit with a change in the structure of the music.

ALIGNING HIT POINTS

Ultimately, the creative team will have to make decisions about how to best align musical ideas with the timings of a scene. Composers and music editors have a variety of software programs and tools available to help with this task. Nonetheless, there are multiple acceptable answers in most cases, and the creative team will have to choose a preferred solution. Let's propose a hypothetical situation and discuss possible solutions.

The composer is brainstorming initial ideas for the scene by improvising at a keyboard while watching the picture. Ultimately, the composer comes to a preferred musical idea. The idea is in 4/4 meter, and the tempo is 92 beats per minute. The film uses a frame rate of 24 frames per second.

Once the composer chooses a tempo and meter, the beats of the music align with certain frames in the picture. The composer need not calculate the timing location of every measure and beat. However, the composer needs to identify visual events that will be synchronization points and locate those timings within the rhythmic structure of the music.

Let's suppose the scene contains a hard picture cut at second 11 frame 11. In real time, this frame begins 11.45 seconds into the scene. The composer enters this information into the computer, which shows that the picture cut falls just after the upbeat of measure 5, beat 2. Assuming the composer wants an exact hit on the cut, there a several options.

Option 1: Use syncopation to accent the upbeat of measure 5, beat 2. Syncopation occurs when a traditionally weak rhythmic location in the measure is accented. In 4/4 meter, beat 1 is the strongest beat of the measure. Beats 1 and 3 are stronger than beats 2 and 4. Likewise, each beat is stronger than the eighth-note subdivision within each beat. Nonetheless, it is not necessary or even desirable to place every musical hit on beat 1 of the measure. Rather, it can be musically exciting to accent the traditionally weaker moments within a measure, creating a rhythmic surprise for the listener. In this case, the picture cut is closest to the eighth-note subdivision of beat 2. At that moment, the composer could create an accent, change the instrumentation, start a melody, or create a harmonic shift.

In this situation, a question inevitably arises: how close is close enough? In this case, the picture cut is slightly after the eighth-note subdivision of beat 2. Will the audience feel the musical hit is early? In general, audiences only notice timing discrepancies that exceed two picture frames. When the frame rate is 24 frames per second, the duration of two frames is 1/12th or 0.083333 of a second. Assuming a tempo of 92 beats per minute and 4/4 meter, then the second eighth note of measure 5 beat 2 arrives 11.41 seconds into the cue, just before second 11 frame 10. In this case, our target picture cut occurs at 11.45 seconds, which is only 0.04 seconds after our desired musical event and within our margin of error. This scenario is shown in musical notation in figure 7.1.

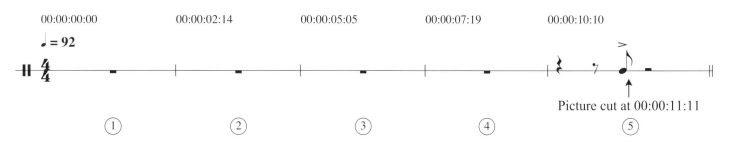

FIG. 7.1. Using Syncopation to Hit a Sync Point

The 2-frame margin of error should not be exceeded with exact hits—a hard picture cut timed with an aggressive musical accent. However, the creative team can use their best judgment in the case of softer synchronization points. Suppose the picture cut uses a gradual crossfade and the musical event is a soft string entrance. In this case, a slightly larger timing discrepancy can still feel natural and convincing to the audience. In such cases, it may not be necessary to use extreme measures to get within the 2-frame margin of error.

Option 2: Change meter to place the picture cut on a downbeat. In this case, the composer's initial idea is in 4/4 meter, which places each downbeat at a certain timing in the scene. Of course, if a different meter is used, then the downbeats will fall at different timing locations. In this case, using 7/8 meter is a viable alternative to 4/4 meter. There are 7 eighth notes in 7/8 meter, whereas 4/4 meter has 8 eighth notes. In essence, each measure is slightly shorter, so each downbeat comes at an earlier point in time. As it happens, if the creative team retains the tempo of 92 beats per minute but switches to 7/8 meter, then the picture cut at second 11 frame 11 falls on the downbeat of measure 6. This scenario is shown in figure 7.2. Such a solution may be optimal if the scene has a chase or action component, a plot situation often paired with musical ideas in 7/8 meter.

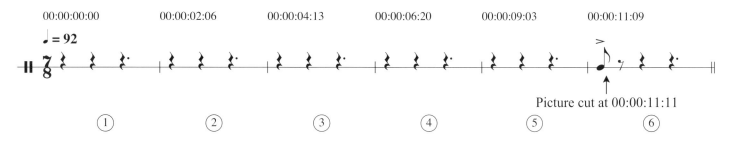

FIG. 7.2. Using a Different Meter to Hit a Sync Point

Similarly, the creative team could choose to change meter for only one measure. If measures 1–4 are in 4/4 meter and measure 5 is in 3/8 meter, then the picture cut falls on the downbeat of measure 6. This scenario is shown in figure 7.3. Often, a short measure placed at the end of a musical phrase can feel quite natural, being heard as a simple extension of the phrase. Here, it may be that measures 1–4 are a traditional four-bar phrase, the single measure of 3/8 temporarily extends that phrase, and then a new phrase begins in measure 6. Best of all, that new phrase is timed to start on the target picture cut. Considering alternate meter structures can assist the creative team with aligning timings— and also lead to interesting and creative musical ideas.

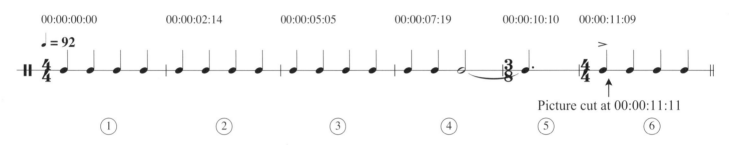

FIG. 7.3. Using a Meter Change to Hit a Sync Point

Option 3: Add a pickup to place the picture cut on a downbeat. A pickup is a partial measure located to the beginning of the phrase. Using a pickup changes the location of each downbeat in the timings of the scene. In this case, adding a pickup that is three eighth notes in duration places the target picture cut on a downbeat. This scenario is shown in figure 7.4.

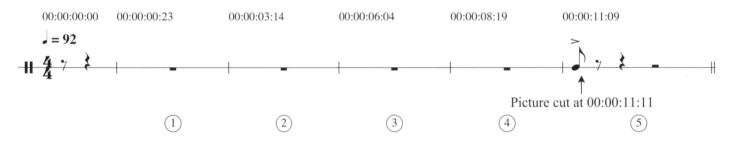

FIG. 7.4. Using a Pickup to Hit a Sync Point

Option 4: Offset the start time of the cue. Suppose the creative team prefers the initial tempo and meter structure, but they want the picture cut to fall on the downbeat. This may be possible if they are willing to start the cue at a slightly later point in time. If the cue is started exactly one second later, then the picture cut occurs at second 10 frame 11 in the timeline. Assuming the creative team retains the 4/4 meter and 92 bpm tempo, then the picture cut now falls on measure 5 beat 1. In this case, changing the start time of the cue creates a natural four-bar phrase before the target picture cut.

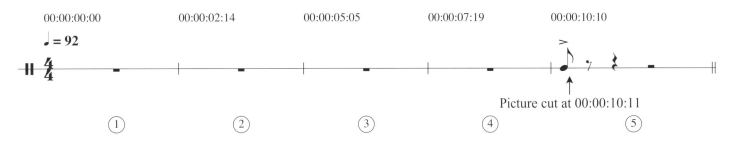

FIG. 7.5. Offsetting the Start Time to Hit a Sync Point

Option 5: Change the tempo. Just as changing the meter relocates each down-beat, changing the tempo realigns where each beat falls in the timeline. In addition, current software programs allow for the use of precise tempo markings, which facilitates extremely accurate synchronization. In this case, if the tempo is changed to 89.02 beats per minute, then the picture cut falls exactly on measure 5 beat 2. Likewise, the tempo 83.78 beats per minute places the picture cut exactly on measure 5 beat 1.

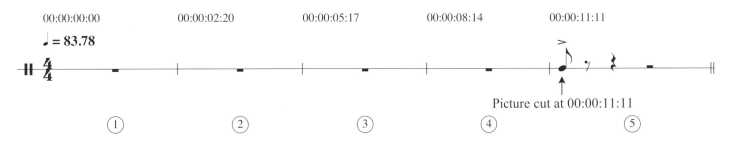

FIG. 7.6. Changing Tempo to Hit a Sync Point

In cases where a scene contains only one hard synchronization point, changing the tempo can be a practical solution. However, when a scene contains multiple synchronization points, the creative team should hesitate before using tempo changes to perfectly align each timing event. Truth be told, the method works wonders on a computer. A new tempo can be chosen at each synchronization point that places the subsequent synchronization point exactly on a beat. Assuming the tempo changes are subtle, listeners are unlikely to feel anything is amiss. Unfortunately, when the music leaves a computer and involves recording live musicians, this technique becomes problematic. Asking a single musician to play along to an ever-evolving tempo can be challenging. Asking a full orchestra to do so is exponentially more problematic. As a result, composers should be extremely cautious about using multiple tempo changes to aid synchronization. Syncopation, meter changes, and offsetting start times are equally effective methods and present fewer problems when recording live musicians.

Overall, there is more than one solution to the challenge presented. The creative team should evaluate various options and choose the method they feel best supports the scene.

SPECIAL CONSIDERATIONS

Before discussing specific examples, let's look at a few special circumstances that come up in regards to contour.

Change the music before or after key lines of dialogue. Significant lines of dialogue are often shifts in contour. However, in no circumstances should the music change at precisely the same time as the important line of dialogue. Change in the music attracts attention to the music, which draws attention away from the dialogue. Rather, the music should change just before or after the key line of dialogue. Often, there will be a picture cut several seconds before the line of dialogue, perhaps a picture cut that reveals the character about to speak. In this case, the cut preceding the dialogue can be hit with a cadence or initiate a sustained texture. After the line of dialogue is delivered, the music can shift to a new idea that reflects how the dialogue changed the plot. Again, there may be a picture cut after the line of dialogue that can facilitate the entrance of a new musical idea.

Precede large hits with reduced instrumentation. Action music often uses large instrumentation. Often in action scenes, a picture cut will reveal a dramatic event, and the creative team will want a large musical accent on that cut. When large instrumentation precedes an accent, the accent is barely noticeable. Rather, the creative team should back up several seconds before the picture cut and reduce the instrumentation. Then, on the picture cut, the music can expand up to full instrumentation. By preceding the large hit with reduced instrumentation, the accent will have greater impact.

Match the duration of the musical idea with the duration of the visual event. There are a variety of effects that the creative team may choose to hit with a musical idea. These effects come in varying lengths, and the creative team can tailor the musical idea to the duration of the corresponding event. For instance, a short pause in the dialogue may be no longer than one second. Such a pause could be filled with a percussion hit or short musical sting. A longer pause in the dialogue may be several seconds, which could be filled with a short melodic line such as several notes of a horn melody. Some visual effects, such as a gradual zoom out, take place over many seconds. These effects can be matched by musical ideas that also take many seconds, such as a slow glissando in strings or a gradual crescendo. When a picture cut initiates a new section or storyline in the plot, it's an opportunity to introduce a new musical idea on the picture cut. When the cut is a hard cut—an instantaneous shift to a new image—the new musical idea can be accented with a cymbal crash or other crisp attack instrument. When the cut is a gradual crossfade, the new musical idea can be initiated with a string instrument or other soft attack instrument.

Differentiate between following the contour and Mickey Mousing. "Mickey Mousing" is extreme synchronization, following every little twist and turn in the picture. Typically, Mickey Mousing is used to mimic on-screen physical move-ment. When a character falls to the ground and the music matches that movement with a descending scale into a percussion crash, that is Mickey Mousing. Mickey Mousing was pervasive in early animation, hence the origination of the term. Today, Mickey Mousing remains common in select genres, particularly animation and comedy, but it is considered undesirable in others, such as serious dramas. It is important to note that most of the techniques discussed here are different from Mickey Mousing. If the main character dies and the music shifts to sad harmonies, that alone is not Mickey Mousing. That is simply following the emotional contour of the story, which is required for effective scoring in all styles. To be considered Mickey Mousing, the synchronization must be both extreme and mimic the physical movement of on-screen events.

HITS IN *THE MATRIX* OPEN

When discussing contour, it ultimately becomes necessary to analyze a specific example, when and how the picture changes, and how those changes are enhanced by shifts in the music. For the next section, we will discuss contour choices in the opening sequence of *The Matrix*, scored by Don Davis. The sequence first states the film studio, production company, and film title. Next, the audience is introduced to the character Trinity, who subsequently undergoes a dramatic chase sequence where she escapes from policemen and agents in suits.

For this section, we will note specific timings in the scene and observe how the picture and music change at those points. You will get the most out of reading this section by first viewing the opening seven minutes of the film.

TIMING	CONTOUR
0:00	The film begins with the Warner Brothers logo. Musically, one of the primary ideas of the score is introduced—alternating minor triads in horns and trumpets. Each triad swells up and down dynamically. While this idea is not a melody per se, it has a similar function in the music. It's a clearly recognizable musical idea that the audience traces throughout the film. The brass elements are accompanied by sustained strings and trill figures in piano and woodwinds. The accompaniment establishes E as tonic, using E minor as the initial chord and a sustained E in the lowest bass. Collectively, these ideas create an initial style, emotion, and energy level for the opening of the film. In terms of contour, they are the point of departure from which the music evolves, going forward.
0:17	The picture changes to the Village Roadshow Pictures logo. The beginning of the logo is matched with a subtle strike in low-register percussion and the entrance of eerie tone colors such as waterphone. As the logo progresses, the percussion and brass fade out, shifting the listener's attention to rhythmic strings and woodwinds. While not traditionally melodic, these fast rhythms are an important idea in the overall score, and the audience recognizes them as they recur throughout the film. Overall, these changes create an initial increase in instrumentation at the beginning of the logo and then a decrease in instrumentation as the logo proceeds. In addition, they create changes in foreground tone color as our attention shifts from the brass swells to the eerie waterphone and then to rhythmic strings. The rhythmic strings represent the introduction of a new motivic idea. Lastly, the string and woodwind rhythms create a subtle increase in rhythmic activity.

TIMING	CONTOUR
0:31	The graphics change to descending text characters. Notably, during the previous logo, the brass and percussion faded down dynamically. Doing so presents an opportunity going forward—the brass and percussion can reenter to create another change in the music. Sure enough, the brass and percussion begin a crescendo just before the descending text appears, and they come to a climactic hit right on the synchronization point. In addition, the rhythmic strings move to a higher register and the sustained E in the bass exits. In all, there are changes in instrumentation, foreground tone color, pitch register, and dynamics at this point.
0:37	The film's title "The Matrix" appears. Previously, the music had removed the brass and then had it reenter to create an impact point. A similar concept of removal and reentrance is used at the main title card. In this case, the low register E was removed during the previous section. On the film's title graphics, the low E reenters. In this case, the reentrance of the low E feels very much like a harmonic resolution to tonic. The moment is accented with a crescendo and hit in percussion, which creates an increase in overall instrumentation. In this case, the shift in the music includes an important harmonic arrival and increase in instrumentation.
0:41	The blinking cursor appears. At this moment, the music shifts to fast rhythms in woodwinds while the sustained E in the low register is held over from the previous section. Here, the overall instrumentation becomes much smaller as the brass and percussion exit. In most cases, the effect of the reduced instrumentation is reinforced by reducing dynamic markings in the musician's parts. The shift to the woodwinds creates a change in foreground tone color. Last, the rhythmic subdivision increases significantly.
0:48	The blinking cursor changes to computer text documenting a phone call and dialogue starts. This is the first dialogue of the film. Musically, the woodwinds and sustained bass both exit, reducing the instrumentation. The small instrumentation ensures the music remains behind the dialogue. The rhythmic ideas previously in the woodwinds move to soft strings in the mid register. The shift from woodwinds to strings creates a change in foreground tone color.
0:53	The graphics change to descending numbers. The camera zooms in, gradually increasing the size of the text. In the dialogue, Trinity has a phone conversation with the character Cypher. Musically, the rhythmic strings are incrementally layered, increasing from mid-register strings to the full string family. Simultaneously, soft woodwinds join the texture. During this section, the overall instrumentation gradually increases. In addition, by expanding to include the upper register strings, the music expands in overall pitch register. Brass and percussion are not used, and the performance dynamics remain low. This ensures the music remains behind the dialogue.
1:17	The dialogue stops. The graphics change from numbers to abstract images that suggest electrical currents. Musically, the initial idea of alternating brass swells returns. The brass and percussion reenter, creating an increase in overall instrumentation. Increasing instrumentation is appropriate when dialogue stops. In addition, the reentrance of the brass creates a shift in tone color as the audience's focus moves from strings to brass.
1:28	The picture is consumed with a flash of bright light. The camera pulls back, revealing the light to be a policeman's flashlight. Musically, the fast rhythms that dominated previous sections stop. The music shifts to sustained and eerie textures, such as bowed metallic percussion. The sustained textures shift tonic to C♯. The initial flash is timed with a musical accent that concludes the previous section, after which the music shifts to smaller instrumentation. During this section, the reduction in instrumentation and rhythmic activity significantly lowers the energy level of the music. Doing so sets up the rest of the scene, allowing the music to expand when the plot turns to action.
1:48	The policemen pause outside of Trinity's door. The music introduces a suspenseful line in upper register violins. The line shifts the listener's attention from the eerie effects to the violins. The violins perform an ascending minor second, a traditionally dissonant interval commonly used to create tension. This interval is used melodically throughout the score.

TIMING	CONTOUR
1:53	The policemen knock down the door and burst into the room. Just for a moment, the visual energy increases significantly as the on-screen characters rush around. Musically, the event is accented with a percussion roll and hit. In addition, a dissonant chord enters in the horns while the upper register violins exit. These changes create an increase in instrumentation, increase in dynamics, shift in foreground instrumentation, and change in overall pitch register.
1:57	A picture cut moves the image to Trinity sitting in the room. This is a drop in visual energy as Trinity is not moving and the policemen pause once in the room. Musically, the upper register violins reenter and the dissonant horn chord exits. These changes decrease the overall instrumentation, shift the foreground instrumentation to violins, and raise the overall pitch register.
2:02	Trinity raises her hands in mock surrender. This moment initiates a crescendo in dissonant trumpets and suspended cymbals.
2:04	A picture cut moves the camera outside of the hotel. Musically, this moment is inherently linked to the previous timing. At 2:02, a crescendo in trumpets and percussion began. At 2:04, the crescendo reaches its peak. The climax is accented by a hit in the low register and the return of the low E in the bass. The music subsequently shifts entirely to the low register. This moment demonstrates how two close timings can work together: the first timing starts a musical idea, and the second timing concludes it.
2:16	The agents arrive. Musically, a hit in the low register is timed with the agent's opening their car doors. The hit utilizes low register percussion and winds, creating increased instrumentation, increased dynamics, and a shift in tone color. The winds perform an ascending minor second, echoing the motivic idea previously stated in violins at 1:48.
2:20	Dialogue begins between the agents and cops. Musically, the previous hit in the low register fades down prior to the start of dialogue, and the entire conversation is scored with soft sustained textures. By pulling back to small instrumentation and soft dynamics, the music remains behind the dialogue.
2:53	Dialogue stops and a picture cut moves the camera back into the hotel room with Trinity. Percussion, brass, and strings swell up and then suddenly stop on the picture cut. The swell is a change in overall instrumentation and dynamics.
3:00	Trinity fights the policemen. This is a dramatic increase in the visual energy level. Suddenly, characters are moving around quickly. In addition, there are frequent picture cuts and moving camera effects. The music also shifts from low to high energy. The instrumentation increases to full orchestra. The dynamics increase. The rhythmic subdivision increases.
3:20	The fight between Trinity and the policemen concludes. This moment is a drop in visual energy, as the characters stop fighting and the camera effects slow. Musically, this moment functions as the ending point for the previous idea. The large instrumentation and fast rhythms of the previous section come to a cadential climax, out of which emerge sustained strings. As a result, the music matches the drop in visual energy level, reducing the instrumentation and rhythmic subdivision.
3:23	A picture cut reveals more policemen entering the hotel, led by an agent. Musically, the cut is hit with a cymbal scrape.
3:25	Dialogue starts. Trinity and Morpheus have a phone conversation. Musically, sustained notes in low bass and high violins continue. The fast rhythms—previously introduced at 0:17—return in mid-register strings. Notably, this is an increase in the rhythmic subdivision, a rare choice when dialogue is starting. In this case, the choice works for several reasons. First, the instrumentation remains small, with no percussion or brass. Second, the dynamics remain soft. Third, the rhythmic strings are predictable in rhythmic and pitch pattern, which helps them remain in the background.

TIMING	CONTOUR
3:44	Just after Morpheus says "Go!" the dialogue stops, and Trinity starts running. Visually, this is an increase in the energy level. Musically, the fast rhythms shift from strings to forte piano. The high violin note exits. These changes create a shift in foreground instrumentation and an increase in dynamics. Increased dynamics are appropriate both because the visual energy has increased and the dialogue has stopped.
3:47	Trinity sees the agent arrive in the elevator. Musically, a melodic line is introduced in horns and trumpets. This shifts the foreground instrumentation from piano to brass, increases overall instrumentation, and introduces a new melodic idea.
3:54	Trinity exits the building on a fire escape. Looking down to the street, she sees another agent. Musically, the horns and trumpets exit. The foreground idea returns to rhythmic piano and strings. Harmonically, the music arrives at a new tonal center, with the rhythmic lines shifting up a step and the low bass now on an F♯.
4:00	The agent on the street looks over his shoulder. Musically, this moment is used to begin a crescendo. Percussion rolls and brass swells are initiated.
4:02	A picture cut shows Trinity running across a roof. Musically, horn and trombone rhythms enter. The rhythms are doubled by hits in large percussion. Notably, the rhythmic emphasis diverges from the rhythmic patterns in the previous section. A shift like this can be created either by changing meter or changing the placement of accents within the existing meter. Harmonically, the tonal center shifts between F♯ and F♮, creating an increase in the harmonic rhythm.
4:18	A picture cut shows Trinity running across the roof in slow motion. Musically, several shifts occur. The rhythm changes, using a more traditional 4/4 meter structure. Trumpets enter, increasing the instrumentation and shifting tone color. The tonal center shifts to D.
4:35	Trinity jumps from one building to another, crossing an entire street. Musically, the dynamic swells in horns and trumpets return. In addition, the rhythmic subdivision reduces dramatically, creating a floating affect that matches the image of Trinity flying through the air.
4:40	Trinity lands and continues running. Musically, the brass exits and the fast rhythms in strings and piano return. The moment is accented with a hit in low-register percussion.
4:43	The agent jumps across the street. Musically, a dissonant chord in brass enters. This moment was made possible by the exit of the brass at 4:40.
4:47	The pursuing policemen stop running. The lead policeman says, "That's impossible." Here, all the musical elements reduce dynamics to get under the line of dialogue. In addition, the reduced dynamics allow the musicians to swell back up for the next hit.
4:48	The agent lands. Visually, this moment represents a drop in energy as both the agent and Trinity have stopped running. Musically, the moment functions as the ending point of the previous idea. The instruments swell up to a forte hit as the agent lands, after which the music shifts to sustained textures. By doing so, the instrumentation and rhythm are reduced, matching the drop in the energy level of the visuals. In addition, the harmony resolves back to E with the return of the E in the low register.
4:57	Trinity sees a small window. Musically, a cymbal scrape leads into this picture cut and a crescendo in percussion starts.
5:00	Trinity starts running. Visually, this is an increase in energy. The music matches that with increased instrumentation, increased rhythmic subdivision, increased dynamics, and expanded overall pitch register.
5:06	Trinity jumps. Just like the last jump, the music returns to the dynamic swells in horns and trumpets. The brass is accompanied by tremolo strings and cymbal swells. The rhythmic subdivision is again reduced, creating a floating texture to match Trinity's airborne status.
5:13	Trinity lands and rolls to her back. Visually, this is a shift to low energy as Trinity has stopped running. The music matches the shift by pulling back to small instrumentation— just a single note in tremolo violin. In addition, the rhythmic activity is pulled out entirely and the focus on violin is a contraction from the full pitch range to just the upper register.

TIMING	CONTOUR
5:26	Trinity gets up and runs, creating a return to high energy visuals. The music returns to full orchestra and a fast rhythmic subdivision. The shift back to full orchestra creates an expansion in overall instrumentation. The foreground instrumentation shifts from violins to brass. The melody here is a restatement of the melodic idea first heard at 3:47.
5:32	A picture cut shows a truck barreling down a street. Musically, the brass exits while percussion and strings remain. A large percussion hit pounds out several beats and the strings play a single tremolo note. This moment is a shift in the foreground instrumentation with the focus shifting to percussion and a reduction in the rhythmic subdivision.
5:39	The truck stops and turns, pointing at a phone booth. Inside the phone booth, the phone rings. Musically, this moment is used to start a crescendo. The music changes to a roll in percussion and tremolo strings, which subsequently build dynamically until the next timing point.
5:43	Trinity sprints towards the phone booth. Simultaneously, the truck accelerates towards the phone booth, placing the two on a collision course. Visually, this is an increase in energy, as both Trinity and the truck begin moving. Musically, the score expands dramatically. The instrumentation expands to full orchestra. All instruments are playing forte or louder dynamics. The rhythmic subdivision increases, as instruments like trumpet play extremely fast rhythmic figures. The complexity of the music also expands from a single chord to multiple lines of counterpoint.
5:49	The truck crashes into the phone booth. This moment signifies the end of the chase. The audience likely thinks Trinity is dead but is confused that she intentionally ran into the path of the truck. As the audience will find out later, the chase has ended because Trinity successfully exited the Matrix. Musically, the score reaches a climactic hit that ends the previous musical idea. A sustained texture in the low register begins after the hit. The sustained texture is a shift in the overall pitch register, contracting to just the low register. It's also a reduction in overall instrumentation and rhythmic activity. All of these changes are appropriate because the energy level of the visuals has dropped. In addition, the compositional structure changes from multiple lines of counterpoint to a sustained pedal point, and the pedal establishes C as a new tonic.
5:58	The agents exit the truck. Musically, multiple low register percussion elements hit the moment with a crescendo into a hit.
6:04	The camera shows a close-up view of the destroyed phone booth. Trinity's body is missing from the rubble. Musically, a harp glissando and upper register string chord enter. These harmonies are less dissonant than the previous music, creating a sense of mystery rather than tension and fear. The moment creates a shift in overall pitch register and foreground instrumentation. Dynamically, the upper register strings start a crescendo that subsequently ends at the next timing.
6:07	The picture cuts back to the agents, who are looking at the rubble of the phone booth. Several seconds later, they begin a conversation. Musically, the crescendo in upper register strings suddenly ends and the peak of the crescendo is highlighted with a cymbal scrape.
6:27	A picture cut shows the rubble of the phone booth. Dialogue between the agents stops. Here, the music expands in overall instrumentation and increases in rhythmic activity. These are typical choices when dialogue exits. In this case, the brass enters and strings begin a rhythmically active motive. This moment also starts a dynamic crescendo that peaks at the next timing.
6:35	The camera dives into the speaker of the broken phone, and the scene ends. Musically, the crescendo peaks and then the music stops.

For the creative team keeping track of changes in contour, the "Characteristics of Change in Music" worksheet can be placed into a table along with the timings of a scene. Doing so creates the "Contour Change Tracker" table in the appendix. As an example, figure 7.7 tracks the first few contour changes of *The Matrix*.

CONTOUR CHANGE TRACKER

Timing	0:00	0:17	0:31	0:37
Plot and Picture Event	Film starts; Warner Brothers Logo	Village Roadshow Pictures Logo	Descending Text Appears	"The Matrix" Text Appears
Instrumentation Increase			X	X
Instrumentation Decrease		X		
Change Foreground Tone Color		X	X	
Change Scale Type				
Move Tonic				
Increase Dissonance Level				
Decrease Dissonance Level				
Increase Harmonic Rhythm				
Decrease Harmonic Rhythm				
Arrive at Significant Harmony				X
Introduce a New Melody or Musical idea	X	X		
Restate a Previous Theme				
End a Melody or Musical Idea				
Change Melodic Phrasing				
Change Meter				
Change Rhythmic Emphasis within the Meter				
Increase Beat Subdivision		X		
Decrease Beat Subdivision				X
Increase Tempo				
Decrease Tempo				
Start the Music				
Stop the Music				
Change Overall Composition Structure				
Change Overall Pitch Register			X	
Change Dynamic Markings			X	
Change Performance Techniques				
Change Recording Techniques				

FIG. 7.7. Initial Contour Changes in *The Matrix*

HITS IN *AVATAR* OPEN

For this section, we will discuss contour choices in the opening sequence of *Avatar*, scored by James Horner. The sequence begins with the camera flying above treetops. Next, the audience is introduced to the main character Jake and is shown images of his spaceship traveling to the distant land Pandora.

For this section, we will note specific timings in the scene and observe how the picture and music change at those points. It is highly recommended that the reader supplement this section by viewing the first five minutes of the film. Please note, there are multiple versions of the film available on DVD and other formats. This analysis discusses the "Original Theatrical Release" of the film.

TIMING	CONTOUR
0:00	20th Century Fox Logo.
0:23	The picture cuts to black. Musically, a sustained pedal E begins in low-register strings, establishing E as the initial tonic. Soon after, primal vocals enter. The beginning of the vocal phrase is punctuated with a bass drum strike. Throughout the film, world music elements are associated with Pandora and its inhabitants. The vocal lines at the very beginning of the film introduce this musical idea.
0:33	Images of treetops appear. The vantage point of the camera moves forward quickly, creating the perception that the audience is flying just above the trees. Visually, this is a significant increase in energy, shifting from an entirely black image to a moving camera effect. Musically, the score matches the increase in visual energy by increasing instrumentation and rhythmic activity. Just as the first images of the trees appear, the bass drum hit returns and a rhythmic flute pattern enters. Shortly thereafter, the percussion expands significantly as multiple large drums pound out a driving rhythmic pattern. In terms of foreground tone color, the audience's attention shifts from the ethnic vocal lines to the pounding drums.
0:40	Voiceover by the main character Jake enters. Musically, the compositional structure remains similar. In particular, the rhythmic flute and drums continue. However, the dynamics of the music are reduced and overall placement of the music in the mix is lowered, ensuring the voiceover is heard as foreground material.
0:51	The voiceover pauses. Musically, the drums and existing instrumentation increase dynamics. The instrumentation subtly increases as a suspended cymbal roll enhances the crescendo.
0:54	The image cuts to black. The cut is accented with a final hit from the pounding drums. This moment acts as the ending point for the previous idea.
0:55	The voiceover reenters. The image of an opening eye fades in. Musically, a sustained note in low register fades in. Notably, the low-register pedal point has changed from E to C, creating a shift to a new tonic. In addition, the instrumentation dramatically decreases, as the drums, flute, and vocals exit. The foreground tone color shifts from the pounding drums to the sustained strings and similar creepy effects. In addition, the style of the music shifts from world music to traditional orchestral film score music. In the film, traditional orchestral music is associated with the humans who have traveled to Pandora.
1:23	Jake's cryosleep chamber opens, and the voiceover pauses. Musically, a new chord progression in the mid register enters, placed in string and brass swells. The chords move in tritones and thirds—from C major to F♯ major and from A minor to C♯ minor. This progression elicits an emotional response of drama and awe for most listeners. In all, this moment uses a variety of musical changes, including a subtle increase in instrumentation and shift in foreground instrumentation. Perhaps most importantly, the moment is a change in the compositional structure from a sustained pedal point to a full chord progression with increased harmonic rhythm.
1:43	A picture cut shows the corpse of Jake's dead brother. The music shifts to a lyrical line in the upper register, where violins and sopranos perform the melody. Here, the shift from the low and mid register to the upper register has a significant impact. Also, the introduction of the soprano tone color changes the foreground instrumentation. Last, tonic is now C♯, a shift made possible by the chord progression in the previous section.

TIMING	CONTOUR
2:10	The voiceover pauses, and a picture cut shows the outside of the spaceship. Musically, a crescendo and accent in large drums highlights the picture cut. Low brass enters, swelling up to forte and then fading away. In this case, the instrumentation increases dramatically with the entrance of brass and percussion. The foreground instrumentation also changes and the overall pitch register expands, now including the low register. Lastly, the sustained elements move tonic up a step to D.
2:19	The camera pans across the side of the spaceship, and Jake's voiceover reenters. Musically, the percussion and brass have faded away, leaving just the sustained strings. A female vocalist enters with a lyrical melodic line. This moment is a shift to smaller instrumentation, as the percussion and brass exit. The smaller instrumentation enables the music to stay behind the voice-over. In addition, the foreground tone color shifts from the low brass to the female vocalist.
2:32	The voiceover pauses, and a picture cut reveals an image of Pandora. Musically, the crescendo and accent in large drums is reused. Again, it is paired with a prominent low brass chord. At the same time, the melody shifts from the female vocalist to unison horns and mid-register strings. This moment is a shift in foreground tone color and an increase in overall instrumentation. The increase in instrumentation works well here because the voiceover has paused.
2:41	Dialogue reenters. The picture cuts to images of officials talking with Jake. They explain that he can take his brother's place on a trip to Pandora. Musically, the large drums and low brass have faded out. The melody shifts from the horns and mid-register strings back to the female vocalist.
2:59	Dialogue pauses, and a picture cut shows the spaceship orbiting Pandora. Musically, the crescendo and accent in large drums is reused. Again, it is paired with a prominent low brass chord. This moment is an increase in instrumentation and shift in foreground tone color.
3:01	Dialogue reenters. Musically, the percussion has faded out, creating a shift to smaller instrumentation that ensures the music remains in the background. The foreground tone color moves from the large drums to the low register strings and brass. The harmonies in strings and brass shift to new chords.
3:06	Dialogue pauses. Musically, the female vocal line returns, creating a shift in tone color and increase in instrumentation. In addition, the pedal point in the low register shifts back down a step to C♯.
3:16	A picture cut shows a finger pressing a button. The button ignites a furnace that incinerates the corpse of Jake's brother. Musically, a prominent trumpet line enters. In addition, the moving lines in strings and vocals come together on a single chord. This reduces the overall counterpoint, creating a change in the compositional structure.
3:22	A small shuttle that has left the large spaceship descends through Pandora's atmosphere. Musically, the crescendo and hit in large drums is reused. The melody shifts back to mid-register strings and brass. As the scene progressions, the female vocal line reenters. These changes increase the instrumentation and shift the melodic tone color. In addition, the pedal point shifts back to D, creating a change in tonic.
3:38	A picture cut moves the camera inside the descending shuttle, showing the passengers on board. Dialogue reenters. Musically, the initial picture cut is hit with a crescendo and accent in large drums. Next, a new chord progression in strings enters while the female vocalist exits, shifting the tone color from the vocalist to strings. Notably, the chords now change more frequently, creating an increase in harmonic rhythm.
3:51	A picture cut shows the pilots operating the shuttle. Musically, a beat in contemporary percussion enters. The beat increases the overall instrumentation and rhythmic subdivision of the music.
3:59	A picture cut moves the camera to the outside of the shuttle, showing its approach to a base on Pandora. Dialogue stops. The music expands. The violins ascend to their upper register, expanding the overall pitch register of the music. The percussion increases, adding large drums to the previous beat. This moment expands both the instrumentation and pitch register.
4:11	A picture cut shows the shuttle's engines rotating to slow their approach. Musically, the violins shift to their lower register and the dynamics subtly reduce. This change allows the music to being a gradual crescendo.
4:33	A picture cut shows Jake's face as he watches his brother's corpse burn. Here, the violins have completed their ascent back to the upper register. Dynamically, the music has reached the peak of the crescendo begun at the previous timing.

TIMING	CONTOUR
4:45	The camera cuts back inside the shuttle and dialogue restarts. Rhythmically, the music slows and instrumentation is reduced. The rhythmic percussion exits. The rhythmic subdivision of the music slows, no longer using the faster rhythms from the previous beat. The harmonies also arrive on new and dramatic chord changes.
5:04	Jake and the other passengers see the surface of Pandora for the first time. The moment is marked by a harmonic arrival that is accented by a percussion hit. Musically, this moment functions as a cadence that concludes the previous musical ideas.

Figure 7.8 tracks the first few contour changes of *Avatar*.

CONTOUR CHANGE TRACKER

Timing	0:00	0:23	0:33	0:40	0:51	0:54	0:55
Plot and Picture Event	20th Century Fox logo	Cut to Black	Treetops Appear	Voice-over enters	Voice-over pauses	Cut to black	Voice-over enters
Instrumentation Increase			X		X		
Instrumentation Decrease							X
Change Foreground Tone Color			X				X
Change Scale Type							
Move Tonic	E						C
Increase Dissonance Level							
Decrease Dissonance Level							
Increase Harmonic Rhythm							
Decrease Harmonic Rhythm							
Arrive at Significant Harmony							
Introduce a New Melody or Musical idea		X	X				X
Restate a Previous Theme							
End a Melody or Musical Idea						X	
Change Melodic Phrasing							
Change Meter							
Change Rhythmic Emphasis within the Meter							
Increase Beat Subdivision			X				
Decrease Beat Subdivision							X
Increase Tempo							
Decrease Tempo							
Start the Music							
Stop the Music							
Change Overall Composition Structure			X				
Change Overall Pitch Register							
Change Dynamic Markings				X	X	X	X
Change Performance Techniques							
Change Recording Techniques							

FIG. 7.8. Initial Contour Changes in *Avatar*

KEY POINTS FROM *THE MATRIX* AND *AVATAR*

In terms of contour, there are many key points we can observe from the opening sequences of *The Matrix* and *Avatar*.

First, the contour of the plot, picture, and dialogue is highly synchronized with the contour of the music. Every time the story changes, the music also changes. In *The Matrix*, there were forty-five sync points—moments a change in the picture was timed with a change in the music—in the first seven minutes of the film. *Avatar* used twenty-three sync points in the first five minutes of the film.

Second, musical hits are created by changing multiple aspects of the music. When a picture cut shows Jake's spaceship at 2:10 of *Avatar*, the overall instrumentation increased, the foreground tone color changed, tonic moved, the harmonic rhythm slowed, and the overall pitch register changed. Musical hits that change multiple characteristics of the music have much more impact than simply adding a cymbal crash to a picture cut.

Third, the musical hits vary a great deal in technique. Some hits increase instrumentation, others decrease it. Some hits increase rhythmic activity, others decrease it. Some hits move tonic, others do not. No two hits are alike, which keeps the music fresh and adds interest to the scene.

Fourth, elements that exit can reenter to create a hit. In *The Matrix*, the entrance of the bass on the film's title card at 0:37 creates a great deal of impact. This moment was possible because the bass faded down at the previous sync point. A creative team can use this technique by backing up to the previous sync point, subtracting a musical element, and then having that element reenter at the current sync point.

Fifth, adjacent timings can be used to begin and end a musical gesture. In *The Matrix*, at 2:02 Trinity raises her hands in mock surrender. At 2:04, the picture cuts outside the hotel. Musically, the timing at 2:02 begins a crescendo and 2:04 concludes that crescendo with an accented hit.

Sixth, changes in overall instrumentation and rhythmic activity are aligned with changes in the energy level of the picture. The opening sequence of *The Matrix* includes a large number of shifts in energy level. Characters suddenly start and stop running. Fights suddenly start and stop. When the energy level suddenly increases, the overall instrumentation and rhythmic subdivision increase. When the energy level suddenly decreases, the overall instrumentation and rhythmic subdivision decrease.

Seventh, entrances and exits of dialogue are used as sync points. When dialogue starts in *The Matrix*, the music shifts to small instrumentation and soft dynamics. When dialogue stops, the overall instrumentation expands and dynamics increase. In *Avatar*, picture cuts often occur in pauses in the dialogue. For instance, the dialogue pauses just before the picture cut revealing Pandora at 2:32. The dialogue subsequently resumes at 2:41. This allows the music to temporarily expand during the pause in the dialogue—and also hit the picture cut.

CONTOUR SUMMARY

Making decisions about contour is one of the most important tasks facing the creative team. Ultimately, contour decisions have a significant impact on the tone and feel of a film. To make effective decisions, the team must first analyze the picture and determine what events warrant a musical hit. Next, the team must consider the wide variety of ways that music can change and select a musical change that best enhances the visual event.

Notably, contour decisions come with a certain amount of subjectivity. Typically, there are events in a film that could be hit musically but don't absolutely have to be hit. Likewise, when everyone agrees a certain moment should be hit, there are a variety of ways to musically hit an event. As is the case with most creative decisions in film, the creative team must discuss the potential choices and come to a consensus about the preferred approach.

CHAPTER 8

Form

Form is a large-scale look at how the music is organized in a project. Decisions about form include when to use music and how musical ideas recur in multiple scenes.

WHEN TO HAVE NO MUSIC

When to have and not have music is an inherent part of a film score's form. There are a variety of reasons to go without music for an entire scene. Let's elaborate on some common scenarios.

Avoid dialogue. In scenes with a great deal of dialogue, it is common to have no music. Removing the music ensures that the dialogue is heard as foreground material.

Avoid sound effects. In scenes with a great deal of sound effects, it is common to have no music. Intense battle scenes are perhaps the most common scene type in this category. First, the sound of gunfire and explosions are often sufficient for driving the energy level of the scene. Second, adding music to a scene with a large amount of sound effects can make the audio landscape overly cluttered. One example of this approach occurs in *The Matrix*. In the 107th minute of the film, Neo and Trinity attempt to rescue Morpheus. They hover in a helicopter outside a skyscraper where Morpheus is held captive. Neo fires a machine gun from the helicopter. Agents inside the building fire back with handguns. The glass exterior of the building shatters into many small pieces. Needless to say, the scene includes a great deal of sound effects. Accordingly, there is no music during the gun battle.

Increase realism. The presence of music can make a scene feel like fiction, while the absence of music can make a scene feel real and factual. When the creative team wants a scene to feel particularly realistic, using no music is a viable option. This approach is common in scenes based on historical fact. One example occurs at the beginning of *Saving Private Ryan*. The opening scene depicts the invasion of Normandy, a factual occurrence during World War II. While the audience watches the events, there is no music for the first twenty-four minutes of the film.

A scene with very serious content. When a scene depicts particularly serious and tragic content, music can risk trivializing the events. In scenes of grave consequence, having no music is an effective option. One example occurs in

Schindler's List (Universal Pictures, 1993). In the 56th minute of the film, German soldiers enter the Jewish ghetto in Krakow with orders to kill all its residents. For the next ten minutes of the film, there is no music.

Scenes with little emotion. Music is used in film, in part, to heighten the emotional content of a scene. Of course, not every scene is an intense emotional climax. For scenes with little or vague emotional content, having no music can be most effective.

The middle of the movie. Most commonly, the opening scene of a film has music. Most creative teams desire a big open that pulls the audience into the film. Similarly, most films have an emotional climax near the end of the film. Typically, there is a great deal of music leading up to, during, and following the climax. As such, the end of the film typically has a great deal of music. By contrast, scenes in the middle of the film—after the opening and before the climax—are opportunities for the visuals to play without music.

WHEN TO USE SOURCE MUSIC

In many films, the music includes both instrumental score and *source music*—music that exists within the story itself and would be heard by the characters. Deciding when to use source music is a fundamental decision the creative team has to make. Let's elaborate on when to and not to use source music.

In some cases, it is absolutely required to use source music. When a character verbally mentions music, sings, plays an instrument or visually presses play on a stereo, source music must be incorporated. One example occurs in the 49th minute of *My Girl* (Columbia Pictures, 1991). The main character, Vada Sultenfuss, has enrolled in a creative writing class. Her classmates Justin and Ronda have offered to lead the class in a group meditation. After giving instructions for the meditation, Justin reaches over to a portable stereo and presses play. At this moment, Indian music appropriate for a meditation begins.

Source music can be used to reinforce a change in plot location. One such instance occurs during the 16th minute of *Apollo 13* (Universal Pictures, 1993). At the beginning of the scene, astronaut Jim Lovell talks to his son at their home. Sun streams in the windows, revealing a daytime setting. After the conversation, a picture cut moves the plot location to the Lovell family car. The sky is black and the car lights are on, revealing a nighttime setting. Jim is driving the car while speaking with his wife, Marilyn. As they talk, a popular song is playing in the background. The audience assumes the song is coming from the car speaker system. In this case, the source music reinforces the change in location and time of day.

Source music tends to be used during less emotional moments. For the audience, source music is factual information. It tells the audience that music is emanating from a speaker system or musicians located within the scene. The style of the source music gives the audience information about the plot location and time period. By contrast, score music is more abstract. It conveys how the characters feel and how the audience should react emotionally.

One example occurs in the 72nd minute of *The Matrix*. In the scene, Neo meets the Oracle, a character who predicts the future. The meeting occurs in the Oracle's kitchen, where she is baking cookies. The scene begins with source music: 1930s style jazz that is presumably coming from the Oracle's home stereo system. After several minutes of casual conversation, the scene becomes emotionally serious. The Oracle tells Neo that Morpheus will soon sacrifice himself to save Neo. Neo will have to choose between saving his life and that of Morpheus. At this shift in the conversation, the source music fades out and score music fades in. The shift to score music reinforces the shift to a more emotional conversation. Notably, a shift from source to score need not be literally justified in the picture. In this scene, the Oracle does not walk over to her stereo and press stop. Rather, the source music simply fades out and score music fades in. The change creates a noticeable shift for the audience, which is justified because there is a shift in the emotions of the plot.

Source music is most common near the beginning of the film. At the beginning of the film, source music helps establish the plot location and time period. By contrast, score music is most common near the climax of the film. The climax, typically near the end of the film, is when the emotional experience for the audience is most intense. Typically, a great deal of score music is used at and leading up to the climax. One example is *Schindler's List*. The beginning of the film uses a variety of source cues—singing in synagogue, a waltz playing on the radio, and tango music at a party. The orchestral score only begins in the 17th minute and is quite sparse during the first hour of the film. By contrast, the emotional climax is filled with score music. The final hour of the film contains a multitude of long orchestral cues, revisiting all the musical themes of the score.

LOCATION IN THE FILM

The location in the film can have a significant impact on the music chosen for a given scene. In general terms, the creative team can divide the timeline of most films into three sections—an opening statement, the main body, and the emotional climax.

The opening statement is the main title and introductory scenes. Music during the opening statement can have a variety of functions—grab the audience's attention, establish stylistic direction, and introduce important musical material. The opening statement nearly always has music, and the music tends to be large in nature. Large music during the opening statement grabs the audience's attention and pulls them into the film.

The main body of the film is a long segment after the opening statement and before the emotional climax. The majority of a film's events and plot twists occur during the main body. The main body of the film affords the creative team a great deal of flexibility. The music can be small or large, slow or fast, source or score. Notably, it can be effective to treat the main body more subtly than the opening statement and climax. Smaller music during the main body makes the opening statement and climax feel large by comparison. Likewise, songs and source music during the main body lend impact and freshness to score music at the climax.

The climax occurs when the audience's emotional experience is most intense. Typically, the climax is located near the end of the film. The climax is not a single picture frame. Rather, the emotional climax occurs across a significant time span, such as ten or fifteen minutes. Musically, there is typically a great deal of music leading up to and during the emotional climax. The music is typically large in nature, contributing significantly to the audience's experience. It is common to use score music and reprise a prominent musical theme at the emotional climax.

Two scenes worthy of comparison occur in *My Girl*. In the 9th minute of the film, Vada and Thomas J. ride bikes together. Leaving their neighborhood, they ride into the local town. The music selected for the scene is the 1966 hit song "Good Lovin'" by the Rascals. In the 66th minute of the film, Vada rides her bike over to Thomas J.'s home and invites him out. Together, they ride bikes around the woods and fields in their local area. In this case, the music is lush orchestral score composed by James Newton Howard.

At first glance, these two scenes are similar. In both cases, Vada and Thomas J. are riding their bikes and the audience is shown the importance of their friendship. However, the location in the timeline of the film is different. The first scene occurs early in the main body of the film. The audience is just now being introduced to the main characters. The scene feels playful and emotionally positive, while the serious emotional events that will take place later in the film are distant and remote. In this case, an upbeat popular song is effective. The second scene is late in the main body of the film as the story transitions to the emotional climax. Within the next twenty minutes of the film, Vada and Thomas J. will share a kiss, Thomas J. will pass away in a tragic accident, and Vada will attend Thomas J.'s funeral. In this case, an emotional orchestral score is appropriate, preparing the audience for the serious events just around the corner.

OVERALL VARIETY

When planning a score, maximizing variety is a worthy goal. A great deal of variety can come from varying leitmotif and other recurring material. In addition, it is beneficial to identify cues that will fall at the extremes of the musical spectrum. What cues will have the smallest and largest instrumentation? What cues will have the least and most rhythmic activity? When scoring the project, the largest cues should be made as big as possible, and the smallest cues should remain as small as possible. Pushing the extremes further apart maximizes variety in the overall score.

LEITMOTIF

When planning the form of a film score, one of the most significant tools available to the creative team is the use of leitmotif. A *leitmotif* is a recurring musical idea associated with a character, location, or plot circumstance. The effective use of leitmotif gives a score a sense of structure and cohesiveness while simultaneously reinforcing the literary themes of a project.

Most commonly, a leitmotif is introduced early in the film when the corresponding plot element first appears. The leitmotif then returns each time the plot element returns. Recurrences of the leitmotif typically employ compositional variation—the material is transposed, fragmented, and reorchestrated to fit the specific dynamics of the new scene. Despite the variation, the material remains recognizable to the audience as stemming from the initial idea. This technique has provided the foundation for thousands of film scores, which is a testament to its effectiveness and ideological longevity.

Leitmotif in *My Girl*

My Girl tells the story of eleven-year-old Vada Sultenfuss, who is growing up in a funeral parlor run by her father. The film details several significant life events for Vada, her father Harry, her soon-to-be stepmother Shelly, and her neighborhood friend Thomas J.

In the first scene of the film, the audience is introduced to Vada and given a sense of her mischievous spirit. Vada has promised to show a dead body to several neighborhood boys. She brings them to a casket in the funeral parlor, only to find it empty when opened. She states that in some cases, the people aren't entirely dead when they arrive at the funeral home. She takes the boys to another room where her grandmother is sitting quietly in a rocking chair. The boys, believing her grandmother to be walking dead, gasp in fear and run out of the house. Vada walks over to her grandmother and sweetly gives her a hug.

The score, composed by James Newton Howard, uses a leitmotif associated with Vada. The leitmotif is introduced in this playful first scene and titled "Vada's Theme" on the film's soundtrack. The full scene includes several memorable melodies, but a particularly prominent theme is introduced at 1:32 of the film when Vada opens the door to greet the neighborhood boys.

Throughout the film, the melody returns when Vada has an emotionally meaningful moment with a friend or family member. It is important to note that the leitmotif is not simply attached to Vada. There are many scenes in the film involving Vada that do not use the leitmotif. Rather, the leitmotif is attached to emotional experiences that build positive bonds between Vada and her loved ones. As such, the leitmotif deepens one of the important literary themes of the film—the significance of friendship and family relationships—rather than simply identifying a character.

The emotional content of the corresponding literary theme determines the specific musical characteristics of the leitmotif. In this case, the musical ideas are sweet and emotionally positive, using a major key, triadic harmonies, 4/4 meter, and traditional four-bar phrasing. The melody is placed in piano and doubled by woodwinds such as flute and clarinet. The texture is completed with strings, which fill out the harmonic accompaniment. These musical ideas produce positive feelings in the listener, appropriate for the literary theme of friendship and family.

TIMING	LEITMOTIF
30th minute	Vada has a meaningful moment with her childhood friend Thomas J. The two are fishing in a nearby pond. While removing a hook from a fish, Vada accidentally pricks her finger causing it to bleed. She encourages Thomas J. to pick a scab on his arm. They rub the two wounds together and become "blood brothers for life." At this moment, the leitmotif returns. The tempo is significantly slower than the first statement of the melody, matching the lower visual energy of the new scene. Only the first seven beats of the melody are used, after which the music moves quickly to a cadence before the end of the scene. Despite these variations, the melody is readily recognizable to the audience.
34th minute	Vada has a meaningful moment with her prospective stepmother Shelly. Vada asks Shelly about her makeup, after which Shelly puts makeup on Vada. During the scene, Shelly talks of her dream to do makeup for Hollywood stars and tells Vada she is pretty. As Shelly begins applying the blue eye shadow, the leitmotif returns. The melody begins in clarinet and moves to flute. Strings and harp perform the harmonic accompaniment. The tempo is slow. In this case, several full four-bar phrases of the melody are performed, lengthening the melody to last the duration of the conversation.
58th minute	Vada has a meaningful moment with her uncle Phil. They watch fireworks from a swing bench and talk about Vada's parents. Uncle Phil tells Vada how, before her mother passed away, her father was quite funny. The moment is tender and shows the personal relationship between Vada and uncle Phil. Musically, the leitmotif returns in piano. Strings again provide the harmonic accompaniment. In this case, the theme is rhythmically changed to 3/4 meter. The tempo remains slow, matching the low energy of the visuals.
67th minute	Vada has another meaningful moment with Thomas J. Vada stops by Thomas J.'s house and invites him out to ride bikes. They ride together on a path through the woods before stopping to rest. When the two are shown riding through the woods, the leitmotif returns. The melody is initially placed in piano and doubled by flute. The melody moves between various woodwind instruments as the scene progresses. The harmonic accompaniment includes strings, harp, acoustic guitar, and light percussion such as triangle. In this case, the leitmotif is much like the initial statement of the material, likely because the scene is long enough to warrant longer phrasing and has a visual energy level similar to the initial scene.
74th minute	Vada has another meaningful moment with Thomas J. The pair sit by a pond in the shade of a tree. Vada asks Thomas J. if he has ever kissed anyone. After he says no, they agree to kiss. First, they practice by kissing their own arms, and then they quickly kiss one another. When Vada brings up the subject of kissing, the leitmotif returns. The melody is placed in clarinet and then moves to flute. Harp and strings perform the harmonic accompaniment. The statement again uses a slow tempo, matching the low visual energy of the scene.
76th minute	Vada has another meaningful moment with Thomas J. The pair are returning home with their bikes. Thomas J. asks Vada if she will remember him someday when she is deciding whom to marry. Vada says yes, she will remember him. During the conversation, a clarinet plays a short variation of the leitmotif. In each measure, the clarinet plays the normal melody notes on beats 1, 2, and 3. The clarinet then sustains through beat 4 where there normally are moving eighth notes. Despite the compositional variation, the theme remains recognizable to the listener.
78th minute	Vada has a meaningful moment with her father, Harry. Vada is in her room feeding her pet goldfish. Her father comes in and shares the sad news that Thomas J. passed away. He stepped on a beehive and had an adverse allergic reaction to the bee stings. As Vada is feeding her goldfish, the leitmotif returns in solo piano. The melody moves on to various woodwinds and strings as the scene progresses.
85th minute	The story recalls Vada's relationship with Thomas J. Vada talks emotionally to Thomas J.'s body at his funeral. Through her tears, Vada says his glasses are missing and explains how Thomas J. wanted to be an acrobat. At this moment, the leitmotif returns, stating two measures of the melody in flute and piano.
95th minute	The story again recalls Vada's relationship with Thomas J. Vada and her father bump into Thomas J.'s mother on the street. Thomas J.'s mother gives Vada a mood ring, which Thomas J. had in his pocket when he died. Vada had lost the ring in the woods. Thomas J. had found it and hoped to return it to Vada. Vada takes the ring and puts it on. When Vada puts the ring on, the leitmotif returns. The melody is first stated in violins and then moves to various woodwind instruments. Strings and harp complete the harmonic accompaniment.
100th minute	The leitmotif returns during the end credits. The song "My Girl" by the Temptations is used at the beginning of the end credits. At the end of the song, the music switches to the film's orchestral score. The first phrase of orchestral music is the leitmotif, stated in its original instrumentation and tempo.

The use of "Vada's Theme" in *My Girl* demonstrates the most common approach to leitmotif in film scoring. First, the leitmotif is a memorable and sing-able melody. By the end of the film, the audience is intimately familiar with the melody and just might leave the theater humming the tune. Second, the leitmotif is linked to a prominent literary theme. The emotional nature of the literary theme guides the musical structure of the leitmotif—determining melodic contour, harmony, tempo, and instrumentation. Third, the leitmotif is introduced early in the film and returns when the story suggests the corresponding literary theme. Fourth, the compositional structure of the leitmotif varies throughout the film. The melody appears in different instruments, the overall instrumentation varies, the tempo changes, the meter changes, the phrase is fragmented, and so on. The variation adds interest to the musical score while simultaneously tailoring the leitmotif to the specifics of each scene.

Leitmotif in *Schindler's List*

Schindler's List is another film that uses a traditional leitmotif. Based on historical events, the film tells the story of the opportunistic businessman Oskar Schindler, who sets out to profit from the injustices of World War II by staffing his Krakow factory with unpaid Jewish workers. After witnessing the murder of innocent Jews in the Krakow ghetto, Schindler evolves into a humanitarian, protecting Jews in his factory and saving 1,100 lives. *Schindler's List* is a story of goodness and hope emerging amidst extreme evil and darkness.

The score, composed by John Williams, uses a leitmotif associated with Schindler's efforts to save the lives of the factory workers. The music is sad yet beautiful, using a haunting melody and minor key harmonies. The tempo is extremely slow, yet the melody uses a persistent eighth-note rhythm. Throughout the film, the melody is placed in intimate instrumentation, such as string and woodwind solos.

TIMING	LEITMOTIF
17th minute	The leitmotif is introduced. At this point, Jews are being forced to evacuate their homes, pack what belongings they can carry into suitcases and march through the streets to housing assigned to them by the German army. Musically, the theme is presented in solo horn and violins. The presentation is very simple, initially just the melody with no harmonic accompaniment. The statement includes the full phrasing of the melody, lasting over a minute in duration. The key is D minor. The function of this initial statement is to introduce the audience to the leitmotif. As such, the simple presentation and full phrasing are important factors.
97th minute	Schindler requests that an imprisoned elderly couple be transferred to the factory. The couple has no manufacturing skills, but Schindler requests their transfer in an attempt to save their lives. This moment is significant in the film, marking the first time Schindler sets aside business and acts on purely humanitarian grounds. In the scene, the leitmotif returns in acoustic guitar. Orchestral strings enter in the second half of the phrase to provide harmonic accompaniment. The key is D minor.
136th minute	Schindler talks with his Jewish accountant Itzhak Stern. They have received orders from Schindler's superiors to transport the factory workers to the Auschwitz concentration camp. They have an emotional conversation where they discuss their options. The scene reveals the personal relationship that has developed between Schindler and Stern. During the conversation, the leitmotif returns in solo recorder. The harmonic accompaniment is placed in orchestral strings. At the end of the scene, the melody briefly shifts to harp. The key is A minor.

TIMING	LEITMOTIF
141st minute	Schindler and Stern create a list of Jewish names. Schindler hopes to bribe German officials, allowing him to transfer each person on the list to a small town in Moravia. As Stern types, the leitmotif returns in section violins. The key is F minor. The leitmotif statement is more fragmented, using only the first four measures of the phrase. Next, the melody shifts to low strings and horns, who restate the same four measures in C minor.
143rd minute	Schindler and Stern complete the list. Schindler reveals to Stern that he is paying German officials for each name on the list. As Schindler peruses several pages of the list, the leitmotif returns in flute. The harmonic accompaniment is placed in strings and harp. The key is A♭ minor.
145th minute	Schindler meets with his German superior Amon Goeth to deliver the list of names. Schindler left the last line of the list empty, hoping to fill it with the name of Amon's maid. When Goeth initially says no, Schindler suggests they settle the issue with a game of cards. When Schindler retrieves a deck of cards from his pocket, the leitmotif returns. The melody is placed in mid-register strings. The key is A♭ minor. Again, only the first four measures of the theme are used.
146th minute	Each person on the list checks in with an attendant. After check-in, they board a train for transport to Brünnlitz, Moravia. As each person states their name, the leitmotif returns in lush orchestral strings. The key is G minor.
163rd minute	The train carrying the Jewish women arrives in Brünnlitz. At this point in the film, everyone on the list has reached safety. Musically, the leitmotif returns in orchestral strings. The melody begins in the violin section, shifts to low-register strings, and concludes in solo violin. For the first time since the beginning of the film, the theme returns to D minor.
176th minute	The war has ended. Schindler, a member of the Nazi party, must now flee as a criminal. After packing his belongings, Schindler says goodbye to Stern and the workers. They present him with a gift and Schindler mourns not saving more people. During the scene's introduction, the leitmotif is hinted at in flute. When the gift is presented, the full theme is stated in solo violin. The key is D minor. As the scene progresses, the melody moves among various strings sections, ultimately returning to the solo violin as the scene concludes.
185th minute	The story shifts to the present day. Holocaust survivors and their descendants place small stones on Schindler's grave. The leitmotif returns as a violin solo leading full strings, harp, and woodwinds. The key begins in D minor and modulates to A minor.
188th minute	The end credits begin. The leitmotif is presented in solo piano before expanding to full orchestra.

The "Theme to *Schindler's List*" demonstrates the traditional use of leitmotif in film scoring. The leitmotif is associated with a primary literary theme of the film. In this case, the leitmotif is linked to Schindler's efforts to save Jewish lives. The leitmotif is introduced early in the film to familiarize the audience with the material. As the leitmotif returns throughout the film, the material utilizes varying instrumentation, keys, and phrasing.

LONG-TERM EVOLUTION IN LEITMOTIF

By definition, a leitmotif is musical material that occurs multiple times throughout a film. As previously noted, each statement of the material varies, employing different instrumentation, tempo, key centers, and other musical characteristics. The variation of a leitmotif presents an opportunity for the creative team. Rather than being randomly applied, the variation can have a logical evolution designed to enhance the emotional climax of the film.

One such approach revolves around the phrasing of the leitmotif. When the leitmotif is first introduced, state a full phrase of the musical idea. In doing so, the audience becomes familiar with the complete material. In *Schindler's List*, the full theme is stated in the 17th minute of the film. During the middle of the film, it is acceptable and even preferable to use small fragments of the theme. In the middle of the film, the plot is unfolding and circumstances in the story are changing. As such, a fragmented musical idea is appropriate. Using only a small fragment of a theme creates instability and anticipation for the audience. With many themes, the first few notes or measures can be isolated as a discreet musical idea. In *Schindler's List*, a fragmented variation of the theme occurs in the 141st minute of the film as Schindler and Stern work on the list. Last, surround the emotional climax of the film with multiple statements of the leitmotif, and use the full phrasing of the musical idea. Doing so resolves the instability created by the previous fragmentation and enhances the climax of the film. In *Schindler's List*, the leitmotif is stated multiple times at the end of the film, including when the workers arrive safely in Brünnlitz, when Schindler says goodbye to the workers, and during the final tribute at Schindler's grave. Each instance uses the full phrasing of the musical idea, creating multiple prolonged statements of the leitmotif at the climax of the film.

Another long-term evolution in leitmotif involves tracking key movement. First, note the key of the initial statement of the material. In the case of *Schindler's List*, the first two statements of the leitmotif—during the 17th and 97th minutes of the film—are in D minor. During the middle of the film, move the leitmotif to other keys. In the case of *Schindler's List*, the leitmotif is stated in F, G, A♭, A, and C minor in the middle of the film. Last, return the leitmotif to the initial key at the climax of the film. In the case of *Schindler's List*, the leitmotif returns to D minor in the 163rd minute of the film when the women arrive safely in Brünnlitz.

While melodic fragmentation and key movement are common long-term evolutions, they are not the only techniques that can be applied to leitmotif. Virtually any aspect of a theme can be changed strategically over the course of a film. Of course, a skeptic may question whether an audience notices such large-scale evolutions. Regardless, employing such techniques certainly does no harm, and a proponent of these techniques can reasonably argue they add logic to a score, heighten emotions at climaxes, and create closure at finales.

NON-MELODIC MOTIVES

Traditional leitmotif are singable melodic themes structured in four- and eight-bar phrases. However, a score can use recurring musical ideas that diverge from this definition, such as short fragmented motives or non-melodic musical effects. Such an approach can have appeal for a creative team seeking a sound stylistically different from traditional leitmotif.

The Matrix, scored by Don Davis, is a film that uses short, fragmented motives rather than long singable themes. The most notable short motive consists of alternating dynamic swells in the brass section. In the initial statement of the motive, a horn swell alternates with a trumpet swell. While it is not a melody the audience will sing along to, it is a readily identifiable musical idea that the audience notices recurring throughout the film.

In the story, the idea is loosely linked to spectacular aerial jumps and visual effects. In the 4th minute of the film, Trinity jumps across a street from one rooftop to another. In the 109th minute of the film, Morpheus leaps from a building to a hovering helicopter. In the 114th minute of the film, Neo and an agent jump towards one another while fighting. The brass swell motive returns for each of these moments. Of course, the motive appears in other situations as well. At the beginning of the film, the Warner Brothers logo is displayed. In the 2nd minute of the film, graphics suggesting electrical currents are shown. In the 16th minute of the film, Neo steps onto the window ledge of a tall skyscraper and looks down. Becoming dizzy and afraid of the height, he returns inside the building. In the 120th minute of the film, Neo becomes trapped in an alleyway while an agent is in pursuit. The brass swell motive is used in each of these situations. In this manner, the brass swell motive permeates the score more comprehensively than a traditional leitmotif, appearing in a wide variety of plot scenarios.

While the brass swells in *The Matrix* differ from the most traditional definition of leitmotif, they achieve a similar end result. They are a readily identifiable musical idea, and the audience notices their recurrence throughout the film. As such, they add a sense of logic and structure to the score.

RECURRING EMOTIONAL GENRE

Many film scores use recurring emotional genre, which are periodically occurring musical structures that elicit a certain emotion (suspense music, horror music, high-energy action music, etc.). The music is not defined by a theme or melody, but rather a more general collection of characteristics—a certain combination of harmony, instrumentation, tempo, rhythm, and so on. Notably, recurring emotional genre can be used alongside traditional leitmotif in a single project. For instance, a film may use a traditional leitmotif for the love scenes but a more general musical structure for the action scenes.

Apollo 13 is a film that uses both traditional leitmotif and recurring emotional genre. *Apollo 13* tells the story of a NASA mission to the moon that encountered technical problems. After aborting the moon landing, NASA and the astronauts solve a variety of unexpected problems to return the astronauts safely to earth.

The score, composed by James Horner, uses a heroic leitmotif associated with progress and achievement. The leitmotif is first stated during the opening credits. The leitmotif returns when the astronauts overcome obstacles, reach a milestone, or return home safely. In addition, the score uses a great deal of drama music, which is associated with difficulty and uncertainty. The drama music does not use a readily identifiable theme but instead utilizes a recurring combination of harmony, tempo, rhythm, and instrumentation.

TIMING	RECURRING EMOTIONAL GENRE
58th minute	The astronauts come to realize the full scale of their problems. Their primary spaceship is heavily damaged and leaking oxygen. Their only alternative vehicle with life support is the lunar module, which was originally intended only to land on the moon. Frantically, they work to turn on the lunar module as their life support slips away. The score uses dramatic music with a medium tempo and moderate amount of rhythmic activity. The overall instrumentation uses strings, woodwinds, subtle brass, and light percussion such as snare drum and woodblock. On picture cuts and pauses in the dialogue, the music temporarily expands with increased instrumentation and percussion hits. The music modulates frequently, using minor-scale harmonies that move around chromatically. An ascending line in the low brass builds tension just before the end of the scene.
87th minute	The astronauts realize the carbon dioxide levels in their vehicle are dangerously high and increasing. Following instructions from NASA headquarters, they work to build a new filter that will reduce the carbon dioxide levels. Musically, the score shares all characteristics of the previous cue, including a medium tempo, moderate amount of rhythmic activity, orchestral instrumentation, dynamic expansions on picture cuts, frequent modulations, minor-scale harmonies, and ascending melodic lines building tension at the end of the scene.
112th minute	The astronauts work to turn on the reentry vehicle, which will be used to reenter the earth's atmosphere. The music returns to the same characteristics noted in the previous cues—a medium tempo, moderate rhythmic activity, orchestral instrumentation, hits on picture cuts, frequent modulations, minor-scale harmonies, and ascending lines leading into the end of the scene.

All of these scenes share a common plot situation. Specifically, the astronauts encounter a problem they must overcome. They work frantically to accomplish a specific task, while the audience is filled with concern and uncertainty. The scene ends with the astronauts completing the task—turning on the lunar module, building the carbon dioxide filter, and turning on the reentry vehicle. Given the similar plot structures, the music should produce the same emotion in each scene.

The score uses a recurring emotional genre that could be called "moderate energy drama." Each cue shares a wide variety of characteristics, designed to produce the same emotional response in the audience during each scene.

RECURRING MUSICAL STYLES

A recurring musical style can contribute significantly to the overall form of a film score. Typically, this approach is most effective when the recurring style differs noticeably from the style of the primary score. For instance, the primary score may be orchestral music, while popular music is used at a recurring situation in the plot.

One film that takes this approach is *The Matrix*. While the primary score is orchestral music, the music shifts to popular music styles at several points in the film. In particular, aggressive instrumental rock is used to score several action scenes that occur in the matrix and simulation programs. While the songs themselves vary, the musical style is consistent in these scenes.

TIMING	RECURRING MUSICAL STYLE
50th minute	Neo spars with Morpheus in a kung fu training program. The music is "Leave You Far Behind" by Lunatic Calm. The track uses a fast tempo, contemporary percussion, electronic synthesizers, bass, and no vocals.
56th minute	Morpheus and Neo walk down a crowded city street in another training program. A woman in a red dress distracts Neo. While Neo is distracted, an agent appears and points a gun at Neo. The music is "Clubbed to Death" by Rob Dougan. The track uses a medium tempo, contemporary percussion, synthesizer effects, strings, and no vocals.
102nd minute	Neo and Trinity enter a tall office building where Morpheus is being held captive. They are well armed with guns and ammunition. After setting off a metal detector in the lobby, a shootout ensues with the building's guards. The music is "Spybreak!" by Propellerheads. The track uses a fast tempo, contemporary percussion, electronic synthesizers, bass, and no vocals.

In each of these scenes, the score switches from orchestral music to aggressive instrumental rock. Notably, these cues are not source music. The music is not emanating from a radio or stereo in the scene. Rather, the aggressive instrumental rock is the score in these scenes. Like other recurring material in film music, the recurring musical style is linked to a specific plot situation—action scenes occurring within the matrix and simulation programs.

CATEGORIZATION AND PLANNING

Categorization is a common technique for organizing large amounts of information. Grocery stores and libraries organize large numbers of individual items into groups defined by similar characteristics. Academics divide all of human knowledge into a handful of fields of study. A field such as mathematics is subsequently divided into smaller subcategories, such as algebra and calculus. This process of categorization allows us to more easily work with large sets of information.

Film scores contain a massive amount of information. Most feature-length scores include over an hour of music, dozens of cues, and thousands of individual notes. Accordingly, categorization can be an effective means for conceptualizing a film score. A leitmotif and its variations, a recurring emotional genre, a recurring musical style—each of these ideas represent a musical category within a score. Most film scores break down into five to ten musical categories. For instance, a score may consist of a love theme leitmotif, an adventure leitmotif, recurring suspense music, recurring chase music, and world music based on the plot location. An effective categorization structure makes scoring a film a less daunting task and produces a score with logic and purpose.

To plan the form of a film score, start by identifying the literary and emotional themes in the story. The most significant literary and emotional themes will subsequently become the basis of each musical category. Next, decide if traditional leitmotif is appropriate for the project. Leitmotif is a specific and identifiable technique, and creative teams are free to decide if they wish leitmotif to be part of their audience's experience. Notably, some literary themes lend themselves more naturally to leitmotif than others. Hero, villain, love, and action adventure themes are commonly prominent leitmotifs. Suspense, drama, and horror music are frequently more general musical structures. Nonetheless, the creative team must decide whether to attach a leitmotif, recurring emotional genre, or recurring musical style to each literary theme. After doing so, a score typically breaks down into five to ten musical categories that form the basic structure of the score. While planning, be sure to weigh other considerations in form. Identify which scenes should and should not have music. Identify which scenes should use source music. Locate the scenes that will have the biggest and smallest music. Locate the emotional climax of the film. Weighing all of these factors will produce a score with an effective form. "Issues in Form" is provided in the appendix to guide the categorization and planning process.

CHAPTER 9

Case Study 1: *Cops*

In this chapter, we will use our decision-making framework to analyze a specific scene. After progressing through the framework, we will use the analysis to create music appropriate for the scene.

The case study is the opening sequence from *Cops* (1922), a comedy starring Bustor Keaton. Before continuing, the reader should view the scene without music. The scene can be viewed at www.halleonard.com/mylibrary using your unique access code provided on the first page of this book.

Video 1v

STYLE

To determine the appropriate musical style for this scene, the creative team should consider geographical location, time period, stylistic choices in similar projects, distribution channel, and target demographic.

Geographical location. The audience is not told the exact geographical location of the story. In actuality, the film was shot in various Los Angeles neighborhoods, but the audience is not specifically given this information. From the audience's perspective, the story occurs in an unstated suburban neighborhood.

Time period. The film was created in 1922, and the time period is plainly obvious to the audience. The characters' attire, as well as the black-and-white imagery, place the time period of the story in the early 20th century. As such, the music should be reminiscent of styles from 1922 or the era shortly preceding 1922. One musical possibility is ragtime, which peaked in popularity during the first two decades of the 20th century.

Similar projects. Cops is both a silent film and a comedy. Silent films did not have a formal musical score, but musical accompaniment was often provided by a small band of musicians in the theater. The musicians commonly drew from classical music literature and current popular music styles when providing musical accompaniment. As such, a small instrumental score influenced by classical music or ragtime would be appropriate.

Comedies employ a wide variety of musical styles, ranging from full orchestral scores to popular songs. While popular music post-dating 1922 would be inappropriate for *Cops*, comedy orchestral music is a viable option. Comedy orchestral music would make the score feel more cinematic to present-day audiences.

Distribution channel. Cops is not a project for a present-day film studio or television network. As such, the music need not incorporate a particular stylistic preference of the studio or network.

Target demographic. Cops is a clever and witty comedy that addresses adult situations, such as unrequited love and financial pressures. As such, the music should appeal to an adult audience. The musical styles considered so far, including ragtime, classical, and orchestral comedy, are effective for an adult demographic.

Desired musical style. Given these considerations, music reminiscent of ragtime and cinematic comedy music is most effective for this project. The music could be performed by either small instrumentation, such as solo piano, or orchestra. Solo piano would be reminiscent of the small ensembles used to accompany silent films in the 1920s. By contrast, an orchestral score would lend a more cinematic sound to the film and feel more like a "movie score" to present day film audiences.

In figure 9.1, the "Style Determination" worksheet has been completed for *Cops.*

STYLE DETERMINATION

1. What is the geographical location of the plot? Does the geographical location change during the film/scene? ___
   unstated suburban neighborhood

2. What musical styles are associated with the geographical location(s)? *N/A*

3. What is the time period location of the plot? Does the time period change during the film/scene? *1922*

4. What musical styles are associated with the time period(s)? *Ragtime*

5. What musical styles are used in similar films and projects? *Silent films - small ensemble. Comedy films - orchestral score.*

6. Should the music be similar to or different from these projects? *Similar*

7. What studio or television network is the project for? *N/A*

8. Is there a stylistic preference at that studio or television network? *N/A*

9. What is the target demographic for the project? *Adult*

Style Determination   1

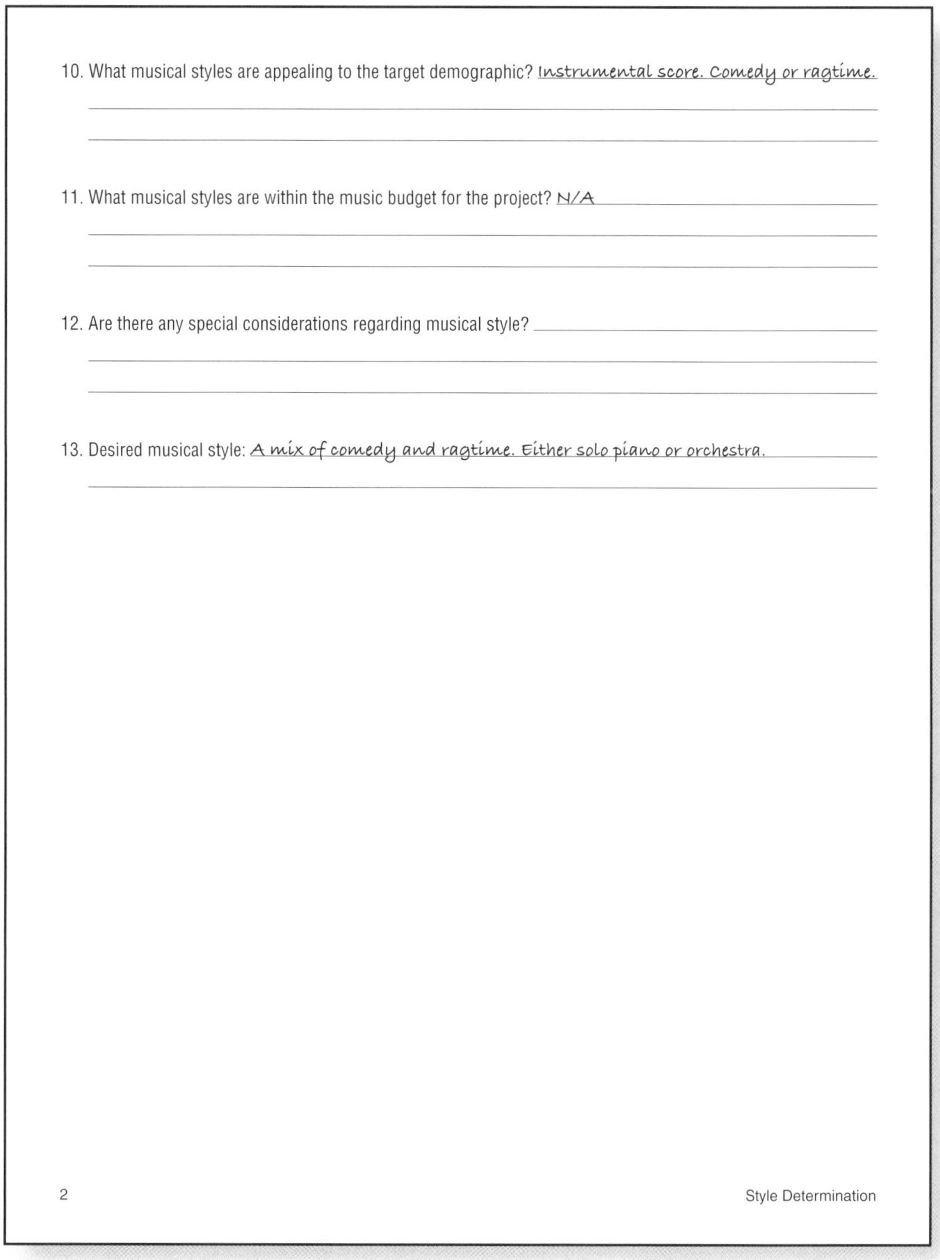

10. What musical styles are appealing to the target demographic? *Instrumental score. Comedy or ragtime.*

11. What musical styles are within the music budget for the project? *N/A*

12. Are there any special considerations regarding musical style?

13. Desired musical style: *A mix of comedy and ragtime. Either solo piano or orchestra.*

2   Style Determination

FIG. 9.1. Determining Style for *Cops*

EMOTION

Emotionally, the excerpt can be divided into two sections—the main title graphics and the conversation. The main title graphics are emotionally ambiguous. The story has not yet started, and the audience is viewing text stating the title of the film and names of the main actors. The emotional content could be nearly anything. As such, it is most appropriate for the music to set the mood of the overall film. *Cops* is a lighthearted comedy. The main character is placed in a variety of witty and humorous situations, and the goal of the filmmakers is to make the audience laugh. The main title music should establish this context, expressing playful, positive, and silly emotions.

After the main title sequence is a conversation between a man and a woman about their feelings. The situation is complicated. The man expresses feelings of affection for the woman. The woman does not accept or outright reject his overtures. Rather, the woman states she would only marry the man if he becomes a successful businessman. The situation presents mixed feelings for the audience. First, the audience senses the personal nature of the conversation. Music that is intimate and emotional would be effective. Second, the audience feels bad for the man. Music reflecting pity, sadness, or empathy would be effective. Last, the scene retains a comedic and humorous undertone. Music that captures the comedic nature of the scene would be idiomatic.

The combination of sadness and comedy is established in the first few shots of the conversation. From the first vantage point, the man appears to be in a jail cell. At this point, the audience feels pity and empathy for the man. The second shot is from a wider angle, revealing the couple to be standing at the gate of a residence. Relieved that the man is not in jail, the audience is likely to wryly smile, even chuckle.

In figure 9.2, the "Brainstorming Emotion" worksheet has been completed for both the main title and conversation. Overall, the music should progress from playful and positive during the main title to intimate and emotional during the conversation.

BRAINSTORMING EMOTION – Main Title

Action	Contemplative	Expansive	Innocence	Patriotic	Soaring
Adrenaline	Contentment	Extreme	Intense	Peaceful	Sophisticated
Adventure	Coping	Fast	Intimate	Pensive	Sorrow
Aggression	Courage	Fear	Inspiring	Perseverance	Spiritual
Ambient	Creepy	Fearless	Instability	Persistent	Strength
Anticipation	Danger	Festive	Intense	Personal	Stress
Apprehension	Darkness	Finality	Introspective	Pity	Suspense
Anger	Denial	Floating	Investigative	(Playful)	Tender
Anxious	Despair	Flying	Ironic	(Positive)	Tension
Attack	Determined	Foreboding	Joy	Powerful	Terror
Awe	Disappointed	Forensic	Laid-back	Primal	Torment
Awkward	Disgust	Frantic	(Laughter)	Presidential	Traditional
Battle	Disoriented	Frenzied	(Lighthearted)	Progress	Tragedy
Beautiful	Distraught	(Funny)	Lonely	Prowling	Triumph
Big Finish	Disturbing	Futuristic	Love	Quiet	Trouble
Bittersweet	Doing Right	Getting Started	Lurking	Quirky	Uncertainty
Bold	Drama	Grief	Lush	Raw	Uneasy
Building	Dread	Gripping	Magical	Reflective	Unknown
Calm	Edge of Seat	Growing	Menacing	Relief	Unsettled
Carefree	Edgy	(Guffaw)	Motivated	Religious	Upsetting
Catastrophic	Eerie	(Happy)	Mysterious	Reminiscent	Urgency
Caution	Elegant	Heartbroken	Nail-biting	Resolution	Villain
Celebratory	Emotional	Heartwarming	Negative	Romance	Wistful
Celestial	Empathy	Helplessness	Nervous	Sad	(Witty)
Chase	Endearing	Hectic	Neutral	Satisfaction	Wonder
Childlike	Energetic	Heroic	Nobility	Scary	Worry
Clever	Escape	Hesitation	Nostalgic	Sentimental	Youth
Climactic	Ethereal	Historic	"Oh no!"	Serene	_____
(Comedy)	Euphoria	Honor	Old Fashioned	Serious	_____
Concern	Evil	Hope	On the move	(Silly)	_____
Conclusion	Evolving	Hopeless	Ominous	Sinister	_____
Conflict	Excitement	Horror	Pain	Sleepy	_____
Confusion	Expanding	(Humorous)	Panic	Sneaky	_____

BRAINSTORMING EMOTION - *Conversation*

Action	Contemplative	Expansive	Innocence	Patriotic	Soaring
Adrenaline	Contentment	Extreme	Intense	Peaceful	Sophisticated
Adventure	Coping	Fast	(Intimate)	Pensive	Sorrow
Aggression	Courage	Fear	Inspiring	Perseverance	Spiritual
Ambient	Creepy	Fearless	Instability	Persistent	Strength
Anticipation	Danger	Festive	Intense	(Personal)	Stress
Apprehension	Darkness	Finality	Introspective	(Pity)	Suspense
Anger	Denial	Floating	Investigative	Playful	Tender
Anxious	Despair	Flying	Ironic	Positive	Tension
Attack	Determined	Forboding	Joy	Powerful	Terror
Awe	(Disappointed)	Forensic	Laid-back	Primal	Torment
Awkward	Disgust	Frantic	Laughter	Presidential	Traditional
Battle	Disoriented	Frenzied	Lighthearted	Progress	Tragedy
Beautiful	Distraught	Funny	Lonely	Prowling	Triumph
Big Finish	Disturbing	Futuristic	(Love)	Quiet	Trouble
Bittersweet	Doing Right	Getting Started	Lurking	Quirky	Uncertainty
Bold	Drama	Grief	Lush	Raw	Uneasy
Building	Dread	Gripping	Magical	Reflective	Unknown
Calm	Edge of Seat	Growing	Menacing	Relief	Unsettled
Carefree	Edgy	Guffaw	Motivated	Religious	(Upsetting)
Catastrophic	Eerie	Happy	Mysterious	Reminiscent	Urgency
Caution	Elegant	Heartbroken	Nail-biting	Resolution	Villain
Celebratory	(Emotional)	Heartwarming	Negative	Romance	Wistful
Celestial	(Empathy)	Helplessness	Nervous	(Sad)	Witty
Chase	Endearing	Hectic	Neutral	Satisfaction	Wonder
Childlike	Energetic	Heroic	Nobility	Scary	Worry
Clever	Escape	Hesitation	Nostalgic	Sentimental	Youth
Climactic	Ethereal	Historic	"Oh no!"	Serene	___
(Comedy)	Euphoria	Honor	Old Fashioned	Serious	___
Concern	Evil	Hope	On the move	Silly	___
Conclusion	Evolving	Hopeless	Ominous	Sinister	___
Conflict	Excitement	Horror	Pain	Sleepy	___
Confusion	Expanding	(Humorous)	Panic	Sneaky	___

FIG. 9.2. Analyzing Emotion in *Cops*.

ENERGY LEVEL

Three text cards are displayed at the beginning of the film. The cards are displayed for a significant amount of time, giving the audience ample time to read the text. There is no visual action yet—no characters or story. The main title sequence has a low visual energy level.

Despite this, medium- to high-energy music would be most appropriate. One of the goals of the main title sequence is to grab the audience's attention and pull them into the film. Typically, large and rhythmically active music achieves this attention-grabbing goal. While the visual energy is a 1 or 2 on a scale of 1 to 5, music that is a 4 or 5 would be ideal.

The conversation is a low energy scene. The characters stand in one place, making only a few hand gestures. They walk away slowly only at the end of the scene. There are five picture cuts during the conversation, which is 25 seconds long. An average of one picture cut every five seconds is a slow pace. The picture cuts during the conversation are hard cuts, but the scene starts and ends with gradual fades. No zoom, pan, or moving camera techniques are employed. On a scale of 1 to 5, a score of 2 would be an ideal energy level for the conversation.

In figure 9.3, the "Visual Energy Analysis" worksheet has been completed for the conversation. Overall, the music should progress from high-energy music during the main title to low-energy music during the conversation.

VISUAL ENERGY ANALYSIS - *Conversation*

1. How much movement is there in on-screen characters and objects?

    1   (2)   3   4   5

    very little   moderate   a great deal

2. How frequently do picture cuts occur?

    1   (2)   3   4   5

    rarely   occasionally   frequently

3. What type of picture cuts are used?

    (1)   2   3   4   (5)

    slow crossfades   hard cuts

4. Does the vantage point of the camera change via zooming or panning?

    (1)   2   3   4   5

    rarely   occasionally   frequently

5. Is the camera itself moving?

    (1)   2   3   4   5

    no   slowly   quickly

6. The overall visual energy level:

    1   (2)   3   4   5

    low   medium   high

FIG. 9.3. Determining Energy Level for *Cops*

DIALOGUE AND SOUND EFFECTS

Cops is a silent film, so there is no audible dialogue or sound effects. Accordingly, the music can be foreground material throughout.

Silent films do employ dialogue cards, which are text cards displayed on screen that state what the characters are saying. During the opening conversation of *Cops*, a dialogue card states, "I won't marry you until you become a big business man." Dialogue cards need not be treated like traditional dialogue, which requires music to recede to the background. Rather, dialogue cards should be treated as shifts in contour. Dialogue cards provide the audience with a great deal of new information, changing the story and emotional state of the audience. Commonly, synchronizing a change in the music with a dialogue card will enhance the impact of the new information.

CONTOUR

The main title sequence and conversation have several shifts in contour. The most prominent contour shifts are noted below.

TIMECODE	EVENT
00:00:00:00	Beginning
00:00:13:14	Text card. "Love laughs at locksmiths."
00:00:20:14	Fade in. Conversation starts.
00:00:31:16	Picture cut. Reveals man is behind a fence rather than in jail.
00:00:35:00	Dialogue card. "I won't marry you until you become a big business man."
00:00:40:05	Woman sticks up her nose.
00:00:45:19	Fade out

FIG. 9.4. Contour Shifts

Each moment provides the audience with new information and changes their emotional experience. Each moment is an opportunity to synchronize a change in the music with the change in the picture.

The main title music should begin with the initial text at 00:00:00:00. The text card at 00:00:13:14 is placed in between the main title and the conversation. Most likely, this moment can be used to transition from the main title musical idea to the conversation musical idea. The fade to the conversation begins at 00:00:20:14. This moment can be used to begin a new musical idea for the conversation. The events at 00:00:31:16, 00:00:35:00, and 00:00:40:05 all subtly shift the story. Changes in harmony, rhythm, and tone color can be used to enhance these shifts.

In figure 9.5, the "Contour Change Tracker" has been prepared with timings.

CONTOUR CHANGE TRACKER

Timing	0:00	13:14	20:14	31:16	35:00	40:05	45:19
Plot and Picture Event	Main Title	Quote	Conversation	Fence	Dialogue	Nose	Out
Instrumentation Increase							
Instrumentation Decrease							
Change Foreground Tone Color							
Change Scale Type							
Move Tonic							
Increase Dissonance Level							
Decrease Dissonance Level							
Increase Harmonic Rhythm							
Decrease Harmonic Rhythm							
Arrive at Significant Harmony							
Introduce a New Melody or Musical idea							
Restate a Previous Theme							
End a Melody or Musical Idea							
Change Melodic Phrasing							
Change Meter							
Change Rhythmic Emphasis within the Meter							
Increase Beat Subdivision							
Decrease Beat Subdivision							
Increase Tempo							
Decrease Tempo							
Start the Music							
Stop the Music							
Change Overall Composition Structure							
Change Overall Pitch Register							
Change Dynamic Markings							
Change Performance Techniques							
Change Recording Techniques							

FIG. 9.5. Synchronization Points in *Cops*.

FORM

Cops is a comedy about a man pursuing his love interest. Along the way, he has several unfortunate brushes with law enforcement, leading to a variety of high-speed chases. Literary themes and emotions for the film include unrequited love, comedy, and action/chase. The man in the initial conversation is the protagonist of the film. The woman and pursuing cops are antagonists.

Traditional leitmotif can be used to add structure to a score for *Cops*. A catchy and memorable theme can be associated with the main character. The theme can return whenever the main character makes progress in his quest—acquires money or outwits the cops. The most logical point in the film to introduce a theme for the main character is during the main title. As such, the main title music should be a catchy and memorable theme that the audience will recognize recurring throughout the film.

Likewise, a traditional leitmotif can be associated with the woman. This theme can return whenever the woman or the relationship is explicitly shown on screen. The most logical point to introduce this theme is during the initial conversation between the man and woman. As such, the conversation music should be a memorable theme that can recur throughout the film.

Notably, the initial conversation is one of the lowest energy scenes in the film. The remainder of the film is full of high-speed chases where the main character flees from the cops. As a result, the music during the conversation should be small and intimate, ensuring dynamic variety in the overall score.

In figure 9.6, the "Issues in Form" worksheet has been completed for the form. In this case, the most important consideration is to establish themes for the man and woman, the former during the main title and the latter during the conversation.

ISSUES IN FORM

1. What are the literary themes of the film, and what emotions do we expect the audience to experience during the film?
Unrequited love, comedy action/chase

2. Is traditional leitmotif appropriate for this film? Yes

3. For each literary theme, is it most effective to attach a leitmotif, recurring motive, recurring emotional genre, or recurring musical style? Leitmotif for the man and woman. Recurring genre for the comedy chase.

4. What scenes should and should not have music? Music wall to wall.

5. What scenes should have source music? None

6. What scene should have the biggest music? What scene should have the smallest music? Biggest - final chase. Smallest - initial conversation

7. When is the emotional climax of the film? Final scene

FIG. 9.6. Planning Form for *Cops*

MUSICAL IDEAS

The analysis above will lead a trained composer to a relatively specific set of musical ideas. While there is always more than one viable solution, all effective solutions will meet the characteristics outlined above. We will look at one possible solution and consider the piece as both a piano solo and orchestral cue.

A logical place to begin is to compose a musical idea for the main title. We can utilize compositional structures common in ragtime and comedy music. Ragtime frequently employs a harmonic accompaniment element that rhythmically alternates between a bass line and upper voices of the harmony. As an added bonus, rhythmic harmonic accompaniment patterns like this are also common in cinematic comedy music. Figure 9.7 shows one such pattern outlining a C major triad. C is played on beat 1 and G is played on beat 3, creating a bass line that establishes C as tonic. The upper voices of the chord—E and G—are played on the weaker beats 2 and 4.

Audio 1

FIG. 9.7. Rhythmic Accompaniment Figure

In addition to musical style, the pattern in figure 9.7 helps establish the desired emotion and energy level. By starting with a major triad, we establish that the music will be happy and positive. The tempo is a brisk 160 beats per minute, ensuring a high energy level for the music.

After establishing a rhythmic foundation in the accompaniment, ragtime typically employs syncopation in the melody. Syncopation occurs when traditionally weak points in the meter are accented. Figure 9.8 reveals a syncopated melody on top of the harmonic accompaniment, which has been expanded to include additional chords. The melody accents the eighth-note subdivision of beat 2, a traditionally weak point in the meter.

Audio 2

FIG. 9.8. Accompaniment with Syncopated Melody

In addition to emulating the ragtime style, the melody and harmony in figure 9.8 help achieve the goals for emotion, energy level, and form. The harmonies use a bit of chromaticism, in particular borrowing the F♯ from the C Lydian mode. Lydian has a quirky and playful feel to it, and incorporating elements of Lydian reinforce the silly emotions of the story. In addition, the melody uses an eighth-note subdivision and mezzo forte dynamics, which raises the energy level of the music. Occasional sixteenth-note figures are added to make the music even more playful. Last, the material has a clear and prominent melody, which can be used as a recurring leitmotif.

Expanding an initial idea to a full eight- or sixteen-bar phrase is recommended when working with leitmotifs. Having the full phrase on hand gives a composer more material to work with when scoring the full project. At times, the full phrase will be used. At other times, only a short fragment is needed. In addition, solidifying the full phrase of the music helps ensure that the material is catchy and memorable. A high percentage of the melodies cemented in the psyche of society are eight- and sixteen-bar phrases, including nursery rhymes, Christmas carols, church hymns, and national anthems. Conceiving a full eight- or sixteen-bar phrase helps ensure the leitmotif is catchy and memorable. In figure 9.9, the material has been expanded to a sixteen-bar phrase.

Audio 3

FIG. 9.9. Full Sixteen-Bar Phrase

The next step is to compose a musical idea for the conversation. This musical idea will become a leitmotif attached to the woman and relationship. Some of the decisions made for the first leitmotif are also relevant with the second leitmotif. First, the music should remain within the same musical style, drawing upon ideas common in ragtime and cinematic comedy. Accordingly, it makes sense to use a harmonic accompaniment that rhythmically alternates between a bass line and upper voices. Likewise, a syncopated melody in the upper register can be employed. In terms of form, we want a catchy and memorable idea that can be traced throughout the full film. Again, a melody plus harmony structure in a full eight- or sixteen-bar phrase will achieve this goal.

Despite the similarities in style and form, the second leitmotif must be different in emotion and energy level. The conversation is sad and upsetting, as the woman does not accept the man's romantic overtures. As such, a minor key would be more appropriate than major or Lydian. The conversation is lower in energy level, requiring softer dynamics and a slower tempo. As an added consideration, 3/4 meter suits the conversation well. A great deal of dance music, such as a waltz, is written in 3/4. While the characters are not literally dancing, they are figuratively dancing, going back and forth and jockeying for position in the relationship.

Figure 9.10 is a musical idea that meets all of these criteria. It uses 3/4 meter and a slow tempo of 63 beats per minute. It is placed in A minor and uses soft dynamics. It states a clear melody over a rhythmic harmonic accompaniment. It uses an eight-bar phrase.

Audio 4

FIG. 9.10. Slow Eight-Bar Phrase

Having sketched plausible ideas for each leitmotif, we can apply them to the scene and adjust the music according to contour considerations. Tailoring the ideas to the specific contour of the scene will involve significant changes and even writing additional material.

Our first contour decision comes at 00:00:13:14 when the picture cuts to the Houdini quote. The quote can be used as a transition, concluding the main title idea and propelling the music into the conversation idea. In this case, setting an initial tempo of 159 bpm and adding a brief introduction aligns the end of the first eight-bar phrase with the Houdini card, creating the phrase shown in figure 9.11.

Audio 5 **Video 2v**

FIG. 9.11. Introduction Added to Align the First Synchronization Point

This is a musical solution for two reasons. First, the main title includes a full eight-bar phrase of the leitmotif, presenting the idea clearly to the audience. Second, a dominant seventh chord is synchronized with the Houdini quote. Dominant seventh chords create a sense of expectation, making the listener want a resolution to the tonic in the next chord. This sense of expectation is effective at transition points, propelling the listener to the next musical idea.

Our next contour decision comes at 00:00:20:14 when the conversation begins. This timing will be used to introduce the second leitmotif, which is in A minor. To get to this point, we can extend the dominant seventh chord to fill the time from 00:00:13:14 to 00:00:20:14. While the dominant seventh chord implies a resolution back to C major, a deceptive resolution to A minor is a common alternative. As such, the dominant seventh chord creates a natural transition to the second leitmotif. During this time, we can abandon the rhythmic harmonic accompaniment pattern established by the theme. Changing the rhythmic

structure of the accompaniment creates a subtle but impactful shift in contour. In addition, the second leitmotif is at a slower tempo, so a ritard during this section will smoothly transition the music to the new tempo.

FIG. 9.12. Transition Added to Align the Second Synchronization Point

Introducing the second leitmotif creates a variety of changes in the music. The key is now A minor. The meter has changed from 4/4 to 3/4. The tempo has decreased from 159 to 63 bpm. The dynamics are now piano. The accompaniment has returned to a consistent rhythmic pattern. These characteristics become a new precedent, from which future contour decisions must depart.

Our next contour decision is at 00:00:31:16, when a picture cut reveals that the man is standing behind a gate rather than in jail. The moment comes as a surprise to the audience. To enhance the surprise, the music can shift to an unexpected idea.

So far, a four-bar phrase of the second leitmotif has been stated. At the end of the four-bar phrase, the harmony has arrived on an E7 chord, which is the dominant seventh in A minor. The listener would expect the leitmotif to continue and the harmony to resolve to tonic, as the music did in our leitmotif sketch. To enhance the surprise in the picture, we can defy the listener's expectation. One solution would interrupt the leitmotif statement, abandon the rhythmic accompaniment pattern, and resolve to an unexpected harmony. Such a solution is realized in figure 9.13.

FIG. 9.13. Second Leitmotif Added

The next shift in contour is the dialogue card at 00:00:35:00. The dialogue card provides the audience with a great deal of plot information, confirming the man's romantic pursuit of the woman and revealing her objections. A musical shift aligned with this new information helps move the scene forward.

The dialogue card comes quickly after the previous timing at 00:00:31:16. As such, we can simply sustain the existing harmony for a measure to arrive at the dialogue card. Once the card appears, we can change from legato to staccato and from a sustained chord to moving eighth notes. Doing so provides a shift in contour while reinforcing the comedic tone of the scene.

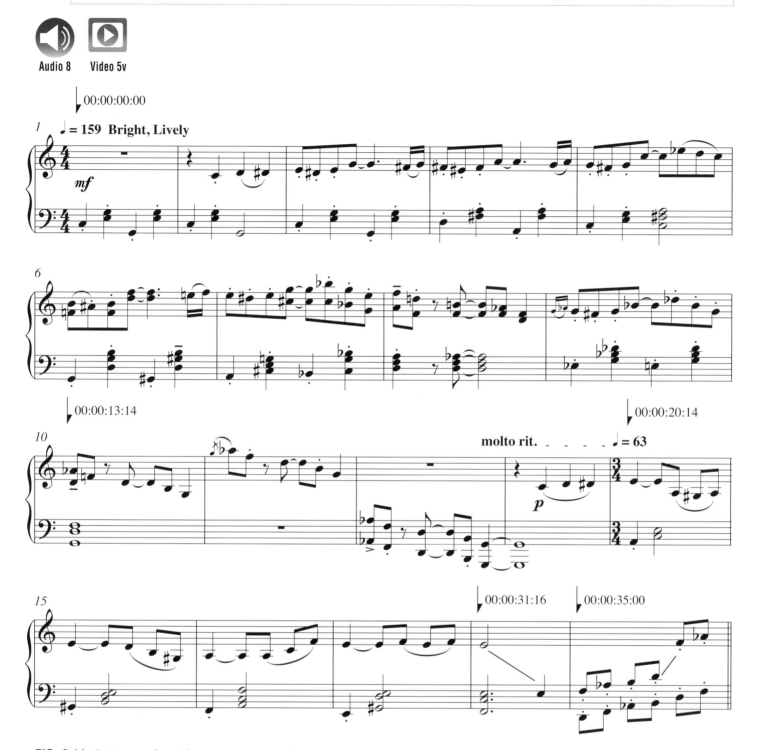

FIG. 9.14. Dialogue Card Synchronization Point Added

Our next contour decision occurs at 00:00:40:05, when the woman sticks her nose up into the air. Hitting this moment would be considered Mickey Mousing—a musical gesture synchronized with a physical movement on screen. In this case, Mickey Mousing is appropriate and desirable. Mickey Mousing was prevalent in early films and continues in present-day comedies. Employing Mickey Mousing reinforces the style of the project—being both a silent film and a comedy.

The physical gesture is a brief ascending gesture. Accordingly, the music can perform a brief ascending line, using grace notes that ascend upward. Of course, changes in harmony, tone color, register and other characteristics can make a Mickey Mousing gesture more impactful. In this case, the music shifts from staccato to legato and arrives on a dominant seventh chord that facilitates a modulation.

FIG. 9.15. Mickey Mousing Added

The scene concludes at 00:00:45:19. Before the end of the scene, we can cadence to E♭ minor. E♭ minor is a key not yet used in the music. Cadencing to an unexpected tonic provides both conclusion and incompletion, creating resolution for the scene while simultaneously creating the expectation that more is to come.

FIG. 9.16. Full Cue

As each contour decision is made, the creative team can update the "Contour Change Tracker" to reflect the changes in the music. Keeping track of changes in the music ensures that each synchronization point is hit effectively. In addition, the table itself can act as a reminder of musical techniques available to the creative team. In figure 9.17, the "Contour Change Tracker" has been updated to reflect the contour decisions made so far.

CONTOUR CHANGE TRACKER

Timing	0:00	13:14	20:14	31:16	35:00	40:05	45:19
Plot and Picture Event	Main Title	Quote	Conversation	Fence	Dialogue	Nose	Out
Instrumentation Increase							
Instrumentation Decrease							
Change Foreground Tone Color							
Change Scale Type	Major		Minor				
Move Tonic	C		A				Eb
Increase Dissonance Level							
Decrease Dissonance Level							
Increase Harmonic Rhythm							
Decrease Harmonic Rhythm							
Arrive at Significant Harmony		V7		VI		V7 → i	
Introduce a New Melody or Musical idea	X		X				
Restate a Previous Theme							
End a Melody or Musical Idea				X			
Change Melodic Phrasing							
Change Meter	4/4		3/4			4/4	
Change Rhythmic Emphasis within the Meter							
Increase Beat Subdivision					X ♪		
Decrease Beat Subdivision				X ♩			
Increase Tempo	159						
Decrease Tempo		rit.	63			rit.	
Start the Music	X						
Stop the Music							X
Change Overall Composition Structure		X		X			
Change Overall Pitch Register							
Change Dynamic Markings	mf		p				
Change Performance Techniques					staccato	legato	
Change Recording Techniques							

FIG. 9.17. Updated Contour Table for *Cops*

In this case, a piano solo is viable instrumentation as a final product, because a piano solo is idiomatic for both silent films and ragtime music.

Nonetheless, a creative team may choose to fully orchestrate the music. When orchestrating, we can enhance some of the effects already inherent in the music. Tone colors common in comedy music can be employed, including pizzicato strings and bouncy woodwinds. The dynamics can be enhanced with changes in overall instrumentation, using full instrumentation for forte moments and small instrumentation for piano moments. The foreground tone color can be changed at important synchronization points. One plausible orchestration of the cue follows in figure 9.18. The score is a transposed score.

Audio 11

Video 8v

FIG. 9.18. Orchestrated Cue. Transposed score.

Last, we can update the "Contour Change Tracker" to reflect the changes in the orchestration. Most notably, the instrumentation decreases and the foreground tone color shifts to solo violin when the conversation starts. In addition, the foreground tone color shifts to woodwinds on the dialogue card at 35:00.

CONTOUR CHANGE TRACKER

Timing	0:00	13:14	20:14	31:16	35:00	40:05	45:19
Plot and Picture Event	Main Title	Quote	Conversation	Fence	Dialogue	Nose	Out
Instrumentation Increase							
Instrumentation Decrease			X				
Change Foreground Tone Color			Solo Violin		WW		
Change Scale Type	Major		Minor				
Move Tonic	C		A				E♭
Increase Dissonance Level							
Decrease Dissonance Level							
Increase Harmonic Rhythm							
Decrease Harmonic Rhythm							
Arrive at Significant Harmony		V7		VI		V7 ⟶ i	
Introduce a New Melody or Musical idea	X		X				
Restate a Previous Theme							
End a Melody or Musical Idea				X			
Change Melodic Phrasing							
Change Meter	4/4		3/4			4/4	
Change Rhythmic Emphasis within the Meter							
Increase Beat Subdivision					X ♪		
Decrease Beat Subdivision				X ♩			
Increase Tempo	159						
Decrease Tempo		rit.	63			rit.	
Start the Music	X						
Stop the Music							X
Change Overall Composition Structure		X		X			
Change Overall Pitch Register							
Change Dynamic Markings	mf		p				
Change Performance Techniques					staccato	legato	
Change Recording Techniques							

FIG. 9.19. Final Contour Table for *Cops*

COPS CONCLUSION

As with all cases, there is more than one plausible musical solution for *Cops*. But all effective scores would meet the criteria outlined by the framework. In this case, the score could be cinematic comedic music or period music from the early twentieth century. The emotion should be lighthearted and playful and shift to intimate and personal during the conversation. The energy level during the conversation is low. The music should enhance changes in the picture changes, such as the Houdini dialogue card and the beginning of the conversation. The music should introduce themes that can be reused throughout the remainder of the project. So long as these criteria are met, the resulting score is a viable musical solution for the scene. In our case, we created two viable possibilities—a piano and fully orchestrated score.

CHAPTER 10

Case Study 2: *Pacific Crest Trail*

In this chapter, we will use our decision-making framework to analyze a specific scene. After progressing through the framework, we will use the analysis to create music appropriate for the scene.

The case study is an excerpt from a documentary about hiking the Pacific Crest Trail. The Pacific Crest Trail is a long-distance hiking trail in the western United States. The trail spans 2,650 miles between the United States' borders with Mexico and Canada. Before continuing, please view the scene without music. It can be viewed at www.halleonard.com/mylibrary using your unique access code provided on the first page of this book.

Video 9v

STYLE

To determine the appropriate musical style for this scene, the creative team should consider geographical location, time period, stylistic choices in similar projects, budget, distribution channel, and target demographic.

Geographical Location. The scene is located in the Sierra Nevada mountains in eastern California. The location is distant and remote, far removed from any cities and urban development. One type of music commonly paired with natural settings is classical music, such as *Peer Gynt* by Edvard Grieg or *Symphony No. 6* "Pastoral" by Ludwig van Beethoven. The music of Aaron Copland is also commonly associated with rural America, including his works *Appalachian Spring*, *Rodeo*, and *Billy the Kid*. An alternative choice is acoustic guitar music, which is often used to elicit rural North America. Given the natural setting, acoustic guitar solos could be appropriate at some point in the documentary. In this scene, the mountain visuals are dramatic and powerful, making large orchestral instrumentation a more effective choice. In this case, orchestral music reminiscent of the compositions of Aaron Copland would be most appropriate.

Time Period. The scene is located in the present day. A variety of musical styles can be used for projects set in the present, including orchestral film music and any popular musical styles. Notably, some popular musical styles are typically associated with urban locations. In this scene, the natural location precludes styles such as hip-hop, while orchestral film music can match both location and time period.

Similar projects. The scene is in the style of nature documentaries such as the *Planet Earth* (British Broadcasting Corporation, 2006) and *The National Parks: America's Best Idea* (Public Broadcasting Service, 2009). Such projects combine stock video footage, still photography, narration, and on-screen interviews to tell the story of amazing natural locations. Nature documentaries use a variety of musical styles, including orchestral film music and smaller ensemble music such as solo guitar.

Distribution channel. The *Pacific Crest Trail* documentary was made independently of an established television network or film studio. As such, the music need not accommodate the stylistic preferences of a specific distribution channel.

Target demographic. The scene targets an adult demographic. The musical styles considered so far, in particular classical music and orchestral film music, are effective for an adult demographic.

Budget. Most documentaries are low budget projects. While many styles are plausible on a small budget, some styles are excluded. Most notably, a custom orchestral score by a famous film composer is not possible on a small budget. Nonetheless, producers of low budget projects typically do not want their project to sound "cheap" and frequently request music that "sounds like big budget film music." As such, an economically sensitive orchestral film score is a common choice for these projects. One common solution is to use orchestral sampling libraries and MIDI software to approximate the sound of an orchestra. Such MIDI recordings can be supplemented by one or two live musicians, enhancing the sound of the music while remaining on budget. Another solution is to record smaller instrumentation than may ideally be desired, limiting the number of string players while using minimal woodwinds, brass, and percussion. Yet another option is to record in a low cost location, such as eastern Europe, rather than Los Angeles or London. One last option is to license orchestral recordings from music libraries. Music libraries place their music in multiple shows, spreading the cost of recording across multiple projects. In our case, an economically produced orchestral score or a MIDI orchestral score would be an appropriate choice.

Desired musical style. Given these considerations, orchestral film music stylistically similar to other nature documentaries and Copland's classical music is a logical choice for this project. To accommodate budget, a recording produced with MIDI software and orchestral samples would be appropriate.

In figure 10.1, the "Style Determination" worksheet has been completed for *Pacific Crest Trail.*

STYLE DETERMINATION

1. What is the geographical location of the plot? Does the geographical location change during the film/scene? ___
Sierra Nevada Mountains. Does not change in scene.

2. What musical styles are associated with the geographical location(s)? *Aaron Copland orchestral music matches nature/mountains in America. Acoustic guitar music matches rural America.*

3. What is the time period location of the plot? Does the time period change during the film/scene? *Present day. Does not change.*

4. What musical styles are associated with the time period(s)? *Orchestral film music, rock 'n roll, and popular music style.*

5. What musical styles are used in similar films and projects? *Orchestral film music, solo guitar.*

6. Should the music be similar to or different from these projects? *Similar*

7. What studio or television network is the project for? *Independent project*

8. Is there a stylistic preference at that studio or television network? *N/A*

9. What is the target demographic for the project? *Adult*

Style Determination   1

10. What musical styles are appealing to the target demographic? Orchestral film music, traditional score.

11. What musical styles are within the music budget for the project? Small budget. Any style that can be produced with MIDI software or licensed from a music library.

12. Are there any special considerations regarding musical style? N/A

13. Desired musical style: MIDI orchestration, similar to Aaron Copland's music.

2 Style Determination

FIG. 10.1. Style Determination for *Pacific Crest Trail*

EMOTION

The scene conveys a variety of emotions. At the beginning of the scene, the audience is shown images of towering mountains covered in snow. The narrator describes the height of the mountains in majestic terms. At this point, the music should convey emotions of awe, grandeur, and majesty. In figure 10.2, the "Analyzing Emotion" worksheet is completed for the opening of the scene.

ANALYZING EMOTION

Action	Contemplative	(Expansive)	Innocence	Patriotic	Soaring
Adrenaline	Contentment	Extreme	Intense	Peaceful	Sophisticated
Adventure	Coping	Fast	Intimate	Pensive	Sorrow
Aggression	Courage	Fear	Inspiring	Perseverance	Spiritual
Ambient	Creepy	Fearless	Instability	Persistent	(Strength)
Anticipation	Danger	Festive	Intense	Personal	Stress
Apprehension	Darkness	Finality	Introspective	Pity	Suspense
Anger	Denial	Floating	Investigative	Playful	Tender
Anxious	Despair	Flying	Ironic	Positive	Tension
Attack	Determined	Foreboding	Joy	(Powerful)	Terror
(Awe)	Disappointed	Forensic	Laid-back	Primal	Torment
Awkward	Disgust	Frantic	Laughter	Presidential	Traditional
Battle	Disoriented	Frenzied	Lighthearted	Progress	Tragedy
Beautiful	Distraught	Funny	Lonely	Prowling	Triumph
Big Finish	Disturbing	Futuristic	Love	Quiet	Trouble
Bittersweet	Doing Right	Getting Started	Lurking	Quirky	Uncertainty
(Bold)	Drama	Grief	Lush	Raw	Uneasy
Building	Dread	Gripping	Magical	Reflective	Unknown
Calm	Edge of Seat	Growing	Menacing	Relief	Unsettled
Carefree	Edgy	Guffaw	Motivated	Religious	Upsetting
Catastrophic	Eerie	Happy	Mysterious	Reminiscent	Urgency
Caution	Elegant	Heartbroken	Nail-biting	Resolution	Villain
Celebratory	Emotional	Heartwarming	Negative	Romance	Wistful
Celestial	Empathy	Helplessness	Nervous	Sad	Witty
Chase	Endearing	Hectic	Neutral	Satisfaction	Wonder
Childlike	Energetic	Heroic	Nobility	Scary	Worry
Clever	Escape	Hesitation	Nostalgic	Sentimental	Youth
(Climactic)	Ethereal	Historic	"Oh no!"	Serene	_Epic_
Comedy	Euphoria	Honor	Old Fashioned	Serious	_Grand_
Concern	Evil	Hope	On the move	Silly	_Magestic_
Conclusion	Evolving	Hopeless	Ominous	Sinister	_____
Conflict	Excitement	Horror	Pain	Sleepy	_____
Confusion	Expanding	Humorous	Panic	Sneaky	_____

FIG. 10.2. Analyzing Emotion for Mountainous Terrain

As the scene progresses, the narrator talks about the isolation created by the mountains. The imagery shows a single hiker, alone, as a tiny speck at the base of the towering mountains. Here, the emotions for the audience shift. No longer emphasizing the grandeur of the mountains, the story focuses on the isolation of the lone hiker. At this point, the music should convey emotions of isolation and solitude. In figure 10.3, the "Analyzing Emotion" worksheet is completed for the middle of the scene.

ANALYZING EMOTION

Action	(Contemplative)	Expansive	Innocence	Patriotic	Soaring
Adrenaline	Contentment	Extreme	Intense	Peaceful	Sophisticated
Adventure	Coping	Fast	Intimate	Pensive	Sorrow
Aggression	Courage	Fear	Inspiring	Perseverance	Spiritual
Ambient	Creepy	Fearless	Instability	Persistent	Strength
Anticipation	Danger	Festive	Intense	Personal	Stress
Apprehension	Darkness	Finality	Introspective	Pity	Suspense
Anger	Denial	Floating	Investigative	Playful	Tender
Anxious	Despair	Flying	Ironic	Positive	Tension
Attack	Determined	Foreboding	Joy	Powerful	Terror
Awe	Disappointed	Forensic	Laid-back	Primal	Torment
Awkward	Disgust	Frantic	Laughter	Presidential	Traditional
Battle	Disoriented	Frenzied	Lighthearted	Progress	Tragedy
Beautiful	Distraught	Funny	(Lonely)	Prowling	Triumph
Big Finish	Disturbing	Futuristic	Love	Quiet	Trouble
Bittersweet	Doing Right	Getting Started	Lurking	Quirky	Uncertainty
Bold	Drama	Grief	Lush	Raw	Uneasy
Building	Dread	Gripping	Magical	Reflective	Unknown
Calm	Edge of Seat	Growing	Menacing	Relief	Unsettled
Carefree	Edgy	Guffaw	Motivated	Religious	Upsetting
Catastrophic	Eerie	Happy	Mysterious	Reminiscent	Urgency
Caution	Elegant	Heartbroken	Nail-biting	Resolution	Villain
Celebratory	Emotional	Heartwarming	Negative	Romance	Wistful
Celestial	(Empathy)	Helplessness	Nervous	Sad	Witty
Chase	Endearing	Hectic	Neutral	Satisfaction	Wonder
Childlike	Energetic	Heroic	Nobility	Scary	Worry
Clever	Escape	Hesitation	Nostalgic	Sentimental	Youth
Climactic	Ethereal	Historic	"Oh no!"	Serene	*Isolation*
Comedy	Euphoria	Honor	Old Fashioned	Serious	*Remote*
Concern	Evil	Hope	On the move	Silly	*Solitude*
Conclusion	Evolving	Hopeless	Ominous	Sinister	
Conflict	Excitement	Horror	Pain	Sleepy	
Confusion	Expanding	Humorous	Panic	Sneaky	

FIG. 10.3. Analyzing Emotion for Lone Hiker

Next, the hiker points out that the remote location creates a uniquely beautiful experience. As the hiker describes the nighttime sky, images of the Milky Way rising above the mountains are shown. At this point, the music should convey emotions of wonder and celestial beauty. In figure 10.4, the "Analyzing Emotion" worksheet is completed for the end of the scene.

ANALYZING EMOTION

Action	Contemplative	Expansive	Innocence	Patriotic	Soaring
Adrenaline	Contentment	Extreme	Intense	(Peaceful)	Sophisticated
Adventure	Coping	Fast	Intimate	(Pensive)	Sorrow
Aggression	Courage	Fear	Inspiring	Perseverance	Spiritual
(Ambient)	Creepy	Fearless	Instability	Persistent	Strength
Anticipation	Danger	Festive	Intense	Personal	Stress
Apprehension	Darkness	Finality	Introspective	Pity	Suspense
Anger	Denial	Floating	Investigative	Playful	Tender
Anxious	Despair	Flying	Ironic	Positive	Tension
Attack	Determined	Foreboding	Joy	Powerful	Terror
Awe	Disappointed	Forensic	Laid-back	Primal	Torment
Awkward	Disgust	Frantic	Laughter	Presidential	Traditional
Battle	Disoriented	Frenzied	Lighthearted	Progress	Tragedy
(Beautiful)	Distraught	Funny	Lonely	Prowling	Triumph
Big Finish	Disturbing	Futuristic	Love	Quiet	Trouble
Bittersweet	Doing Right	Getting Started	Lurking	Quirky	Uncertainty
Bold	Drama	Grief	Lush	Raw	Uneasy
Building	Dread	Gripping	Magical	(Reflective)	Unknown
(Calm)	Edge of Seat	Growing	Menacing	Relief	Unsettled
Carefree	Edgy	Guffaw	Motivated	Religious	Upsetting
Catastrophic	Eerie	Happy	(Mysterious)	Reminiscent	Urgency
Caution	Elegant	Heartbroken	Nail-biting	Resolution	Villain
Celebratory	Emotional	Heartwarming	Negative	Romance	Wistful
(Celestial)	Empathy	Helplessness	Nervous	Sad	Witty
Chase	Endearing	Hectic	Neutral	Satisfaction	(Wonder)
Childlike	Energetic	Heroic	Nobility	Scary	Worry
Clever	Escape	Hesitation	Nostalgic	Sentimental	Youth
Climactic	(Ethereal)	Historic	"Oh no!"	(Serene)	_____
Comedy	Euphoria	Honor	Old Fashioned	Serious	_____
Concern	Evil	Hope	On the move	Silly	_____
Conclusion	Evolving	Hopeless	Ominous	Sinister	_____
Conflict	Excitement	Horror	Pain	Sleepy	_____
Confusion	Expanding	Humorous	Panic	Sneaky	

FIG. 10.4. Analyzing Emotion for Starry Sky

Overall, the key observation is that the emotions of the scene evolve. The music should reinforce this evolution, beginning epic and grand, becoming distant and remote, and shifting to celestial beauty.

ENERGY LEVEL

Like many other documentaries, this scene uses some stock video, still photography, and on-screen interviews to tell the story. Visually, there is only slight movement of on-screen objects. The first image of mountainous terrain includes passing clouds and cascading snow. The middle of the scene includes blizzard footage, showing snow blowing across frozen terrain. The remaining images are still photographs and an on-screen interview.

The scene uses six picture cuts during one minute and 26 seconds of footage, averaging one picture cut every 14 seconds. The picture cuts are all gradual cross-fades, rather than hard cuts. The energy produced by the frequency and type of picture cuts is low.

Documentaries often add motion to stock video and still photography using zoom and pan effects. This technique is noticeably exploited in our scene. For instance, the opening shot of mountains pan across the images, beginning with a subset of the image and gradually revealing the full picture. This technique adds a bit of energy and interest to the visual images.

In figure 10.5, the "Visual Energy Analysis" worksheet is completed for the scene. The answers to the various questions range from 1 to 4, while the overall scene is given a low energy 2 on a scale of 1 to 5. Musically, this means we should employ a slow tempo and use predominantly sustained textures.

VISUAL ENERGY ANALYSIS

1. How much movement is there in on-screen characters and objects?

      (1)   2   3   4   5

    very little   moderate   a great deal

2. How frequently do picture cuts occur?

      (1)   2   3   4   5

    rarely   occasionally   frequently

3. What type of picture cuts are used?

      1   (2)   3   4   5

    slow crossfades   hard cuts

4. Does the vantage point of the camera change via zooming or panning?

      1   2   3   (4)   5

    rarely   occasionally   frequently

5. Is the camera itself moving?

      (1)   2   3   4   5

    no   slowly   quickly

6. The overall visual energy level:

      1   (2)   3   4   5

    low   medium   high

FIG. 10.5. Visual Energy Analysis for *Pacific Crest Trail*

DIALOGUE AND SOUND EFFECTS

The scene has a significant amount of dialogue, including narration and an on-screen interview. When this dialogue is present, the music must be background material.

Notably, there are several points in the scene when there is no dialogue. Most significantly, the scene opens with a shot of the mountains and no dialogue. The narration doesn't begin until 25 seconds into the scene. As a result, the music can be foreground material during the opening moments of the scene.

Once the dialogue begins, there are several moments where it pauses. At 0:32, the narration pauses for a few seconds. There are also short pauses at 0:45, 0:55, and 1:14. These pauses are moments the music can temporarily expand or otherwise grab the audience's attention.

The only sound effect in the scene is the sound of blowing snow at 0:41. The sound effect occurs during dialogue and is background information. The scene doesn't include any foreground sound effects to which the music must defer.

In this scene, the foreground attention of the audience should alternate between the music and the dialogue. When there is no dialogue, the music can be foreground material. When the dialogue enters, the music must shift to the background. Most likely, this can be achieved by reducing instrumentation, reducing rhythmic activity, and minimizing melody when dialogue enters.

In figure 10.6, the "Dialogue and Sound Effects" worksheet is completed for the scene.

DIALOGUE AND SOUND EFFECTS

1. Is there dialogue? (Yes)   No

2. Is there anywhere the dialogue stops or pauses? (Yes)   No

3. If there are breaks in the dialogue, where are they located? _No dialogue from :00 to :25. Short pauses_
   at :32, :45, :55, and 1:14.

4. Are there sound effects? (Yes)   No
   If there are sound effects, are they foreground or background material? _Background_

5. Given the answers to questions 1 to 4, should the music be foreground or background material? _When_
   there is no dialogue, music is the foreground material. When dialogue enters, music is
   background material.

6. The following compositional techniques help music recede to the background. Which can be applied to the scene?

   ☐ No music at all

   ☒ Small instrumentation

   ☐ Soft tone colors

   ☒ Sustained textures

   ☐ Predictability in the musical structure

   ☐ Use a condensed pitch range

   ☒ No or minimized melody

   ☐ Avoid musical tone colors that are similar to the foreground tone color

FIG. 10.6. Dialogue and Sound Effects for *Pacific Crest Trail*

CONTOUR

The scene contains several contour shifts, created by changes in the plot, picture cuts, and entrances and exits of dialogue. The contour shifts are noted below.

TIMECODE	EVENT
00:00:00:00	Beginning
00:00:21:05	Picture cut. New view of mountains.
00:00:25:18	Narration starts.
00:00:31:22	Narration stops.
00:00:32:04	Picture cut. New view of mountains.
00:00:35:15	Narration starts.
00:00:39:26	Picture cut. Blowing snow.
00:00:43:24	Narration stops.
00:00:44:12	Picture cut. New view of mountains.
00:00:45:23	Narration starts.
00:00:51:22	Lone hiker appears on-screen.
00:00:55:03	Narration stops.
00:00:56:29	Hiker dialogue starts.
00:00:59:28	Picture cut. Headshot of hiker interview.
00:01:03:00	Picture cut. Starry sky.
00:01:12:27	Hiker dialogue stops.
00:01:15:18	Narration starts.
00:01:25:24	End of scene.

FIG. 10.7. Contour Shifts

Each moment is a change in the audience's experience, providing new information or a new viewpoint. Each moment could be enhanced by a change in the music.

TIMING	SYNC POINT
0:00	The scene begins with dramatic imagery of the Sierra Nevada Mountains.
0:21	A picture cut changes the image to a different mountain range. Most likely, this cut could be synchronized with a change in harmony or a conclusion of the initial musical idea.
0:25	The narration starts. Here, the music should recede to the background.
0:31 to 0:35	A pause in the narration coincides with a picture cut revealing a new view of the mountains. At this cut, the music could temporarily move to the foreground with an expansion in instrumentation or rhythm.
0:39	The images of blowing snow occur. This moment could be synchronized with an increase in rhythmic activity or a new musical idea.
0:43 to 0:45	A short pause in the narration is paired with a new view of the mountains. This moment is quite similar to 0:31 and could revisit a similar musical idea.
0:51	A lone hiker appears on-screen at the base of the mountains. This moment shifts the audience's attention from the grandeur of the mountains to the isolation of the hiker. Likely, the music should change in harmony or instrumentation to enhance this shift.
0:55	A slight pause is placed between the conclusion of the narration and the start of the hiker's dialogue. This moment could be the conclusion of the previous musical idea.
0:59	A picture cut reveals the hiker in an on-screen interview. At this moment, the music could stop entirely or be progressively fading out.
1:03	An image of a starry sky appears. This moment shifts the story in a new direction and could introduce a new musical idea.
1:12	The interview ends and the narration restarts, with a slight pause in between. This moment could be a resolution or cadence, concluding the previous musical idea.
1:25	The scene ends, and the music should also end.

Fig. 10.8. Changes in Music

In figure 10.9, the "Contour Change Tracker" has been prepared with timings.

CONTOUR CHANGE TRACKER

Timing	0:00	21:05	25:18	31:22	32:04	35:15
Plot and Picture Event	Beginning	Mountains	VO Starts	VO Stops	Mountains	VO Starts
Instrumentation Increase						
Instrumentation Decrease						
Change Foreground Tone Color						
Change Scale Type						
Move Tonic						
Increase Dissonance Level						
Decrease Dissonance Level						
Increase Harmonic Rhythm						
Decrease Harmonic Rhythm						
Arrive at Significant Harmony						
Introduce a New Melody or Musical idea						
Restate a Previous Theme						
End a Melody or Musical Idea						
Change Melodic Phrasing						
Change Meter						
Change Rhythmic Emphasis within the Meter						
Increase Beat Subdivision						
Decrease Beat Subdivision						
Increase Tempo						
Decrease Tempo						
Start the Music						
Stop the Music						
Change Overall Composition Structure						
Change Overall Pitch Register						
Change Dynamic Markings						
Change Performance Techniques						
Change Recording Techniques						

CONTOUR CHANGE TRACKER

Timing	39:26	43:24	44:12	45:23	51:22	55:03
Plot and Picture Event	Blizzard	VO Stops	Mountains	VO Starts	Lone Hiker	VO Stops
Instrumentation Increase						
Instrumentation Decrease						
Change Foreground Tone Color						
Change Scale Type						
Move Tonic						
Increase Dissonance Level						
Decrease Dissonance Level						
Increase Harmonic Rhythm						
Decrease Harmonic Rhythm						
Arrive at Significant Harmony						
Introduce a New Melody or Musical idea						
Restate a Previous Theme						
End a Melody or Musical Idea						
Change Melodic Phrasing						
Change Meter						
Change Rhythmic Emphasis within the Meter						
Increase Beat Subdivision						
Decrease Beat Subdivision						
Increase Tempo						
Decrease Tempo						
Start the Music						
Stop the Music						
Change Overall Composition Structure						
Change Overall Pitch Register						
Change Dynamic Markings						
Change Performance Techniques						
Change Recording Techniques						

CONTOUR CHANGE TRACKER

Timing	56:29	59:28	1:03:00	1:12:27	1:15:18	1:25:24
Plot and Picture Event	Dlg. Starts	Headshot	Starry Sky	Dlg. Stops	VO Starts	End
Instrumentation Increase						
Instrumentation Decrease						
Change Foreground Tone Color						
Change Scale Type						
Move Tonic						
Increase Dissonance Level						
Decrease Dissonance Level						
Increase Harmonic Rhythm						
Decrease Harmonic Rhythm						
Arrive at Significant Harmony						
Introduce a New Melody or Musical idea						
Restate a Previous Theme						
End a Melody or Musical Idea						
Change Melodic Phrasing						
Change Meter						
Change Rhythmic Emphasis within the Meter						
Increase Beat Subdivision						
Decrease Beat Subdivision						
Increase Tempo						
Decrease Tempo						
Start the Music						
Stop the Music						
Change Overall Composition Structure						
Change Overall Pitch Register						
Change Dynamic Markings						
Change Performance Techniques						
Change Recording Techniques						

FIG. 10.9. Synchronization Points in *Pacific Crest Trail*

FORM

When working with an excerpt or individual scene, it is tempting to skip a proper analysis of the project's overall form. However, form should always be considered in the creative process, or else effective musical opportunities may be overlooked.

Documentaries typically use recurring material more subtly than traditional leitmotif projects. Nonetheless, most documentaries use recurring musical ideas that add structure to the project. In the case of nature documentaries, recurring material is often linked to specific locations and plot situations. Perhaps one musical idea is used for desert locations and another idea for mountain locations. Perhaps the hikers face a seemingly insurmountable obstacle at multiple points in the journey, and a specific musical idea recurs at each point.

In our case, the opening of the scene may be part of a recurring musical idea attached to the Sierra Nevada mountain range or large mountain scenery in general. The end of the scene could be a recurring musical idea attached to the nighttime sky or more general natural beauty. When working with our scene individually, our best bet is to create memorable musical ideas that could be reused in other scenes. A memorable melody would work during the opening when there is no dialogue. The starry sky could be paired with unique instrumentation such as choir.

A form consideration specific to documentaries is how to handle on-screen interviews. Quite often, interviews are used to change the direction of the story, and the interview in our scene is used for this purpose. Before the interview, the story focuses on the grand scale of the mountains. After the interview, the story shifts to the beauty of the nighttime sky. Being pivot points in the plot, on-screen interviews are opportunities for synchronization points. One common approach is to stop the music during the interview and begin a new musical idea after the interview concludes. This technique—stopping the music for an on-screen interview—is likely to recur throughout any documentary, becoming a structure idea in the form. Of course, the technique can become predictable when overused, so the creative team should consider having the music play through on-screen interviews when possible.

In figure 10.10, the worksheet "Issues in Form" has been completed for *Pacific Crest Trail.*

ISSUES IN FORM

1. What are the literary themes of the film, and what emotions do we expect the audience to experience during the film? *Achievement, nature, overcoming obstacles*

2. Is traditional leitmotif appropriate for this film? *Yes, but subtly.*

3. For each literary theme, is it most effective to attach a leitmotif, recurring motive, recurring emotional genre, or recurring musical style? *Leitmotif, recurring emotionl genre, recurring musical style.*

4. What scenes should and should not have music? *All stills and videos have music. On-screen interviews frequently don't have music.*

5. What scenes should have source music? *None*

6. What scene should have the biggest music? What scene should have the smallest music? *Biggest - mountain imagery. Smallest - emotional interviews.*

7. When is the emotional climax of the film? *Completion of hike.*

FIG. 10.10. Issues in Form for *Pacific Crest Trail*

MUSICAL IDEAS

The analysis above will lead a trained composer to a relatively specific set of musical ideas. While there is always more than one viable solution, all effective solutions will meet the characteristics outlined above. We will look at one possible solution.

A logical place to begin is to generate a musical idea for the opening mountain imagery. When creating an initial musical idea, we should be sure to create the desired musical style, emotion, and energy level outlined by our analysis. In this case, we desired a low energy level, so it makes sense to use a slow tempo. The target emotions are awe, majesty, and grandeur. In music composition, harmonies and melodies using perfect intervals—perfect fifths and perfect fourths—typically generate these emotions. Perfect intervals can be matched with brass and percussion instrumentation to enhance the effect of power and grandeur. In addition, these types are harmonies, melodies, and instrumentation are a distinctive characteristic of Copland's Americana music, meaning such ideas will match both our desired emotion and musical style.

To begin brainstorming, we can look at the pitches generated by ascending perfect fifths and perfect fourths. Figure 10.11 shows the initial perfect fifths and perfect fourths above the pitch G. Ascending perfect fifths generates D and A. Ascending perfect fourths generates C and F.

Audio 12

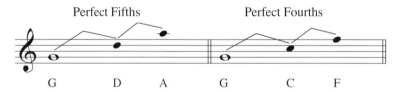

FIG. 10.11. Perfect Fifths and Fourths above G

Audio 13

Figure 10.11 gives us five pitches, which we can use as a five note scale. Writing a melody with this scale ensures the use of many perfect intervals, which will produce emotions of grandeur and awe. To further match our desired energy level and musical style, we can use a slow tempo and place the melody in brass instrumentation. Figure 10.12 is a short four-bar melody meeting these characteristics.

FIG. 10.12. Initial Melodic Idea

Audio 14

To expand on this idea, we can add a counterline in the low register. To ensure the counterline matches the emotional character of the melody, we can use the same scale. Placing the counterline in low strings, low woodwinds, timpani, and percussion would complement the horn melodic tone color and keep the music within our target style. Figure 10.13 includes both melody and countermelody.

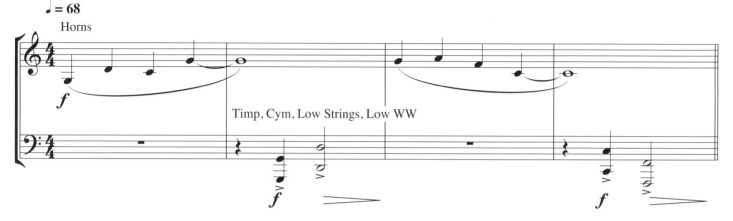

FIG. 10.13. Initial Melody and Countermelody

Audio 15

Just as perfect intervals can be used melodically, they can be used to create chords. In our case, we haven't yet used the upper register. There, we could sustain chords in the upper strings, again using a plethora of perfect fifths and perfect fourths. Figure 10.14 includes an initial melody, countermelody, and harmony.

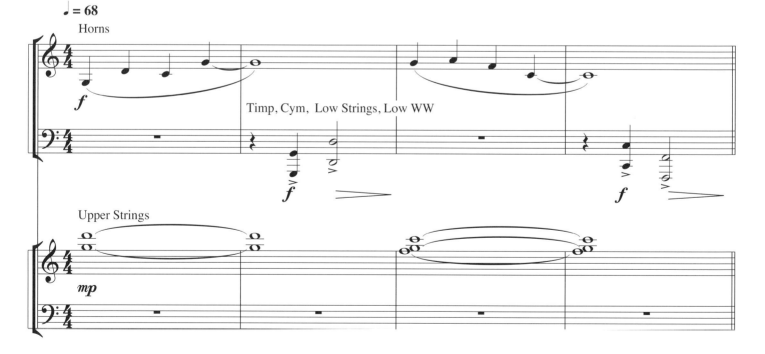

FIG. 10.14. Initial Melody, Countermelody, Harmony

At this point, it makes sense to compare our musical idea with the timings of the scene. The first synchronization point occurs at 00:00:21:05, which arrives just after measure 7 beat 1 in our tempo of 68 bpm. If we extend our material for two measures, we will arrive at the first synchronization point. Of course, it would be wonderful if the music changed in some way on the picture cut, such as arriving on an important harmony. In our case, we can use the moment to arrive on a G major triad, which will have impact both because G is tonic and we have not yet heard a major triad. Figure 10.15 extends the melody for two measures and then arrives on a G major triad. Notably, the dense voicing of the G major triad—closed voicings at the bottom of the bass clef—is a common voicing in film scoring, though it may be unusual in other musical styles.

Audio 16   Video 10v

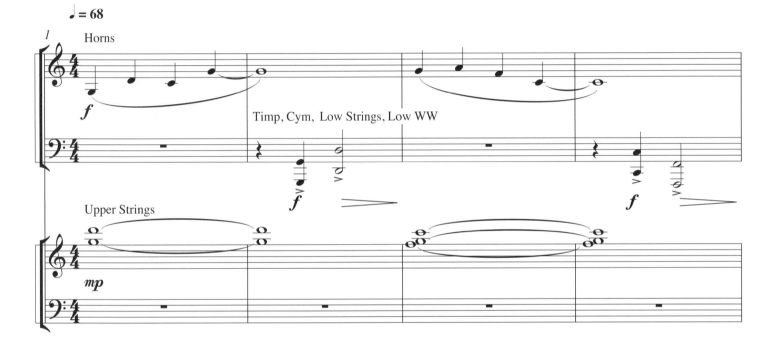

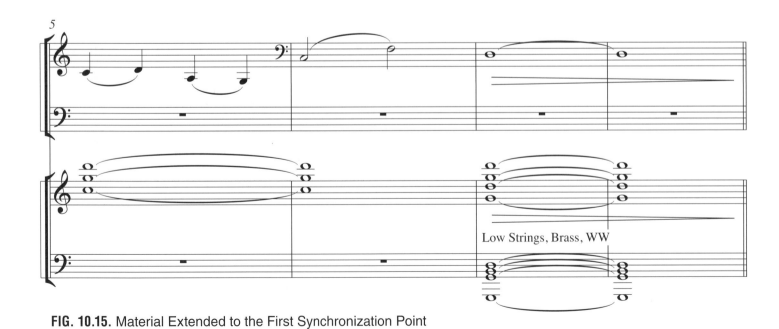

FIG. 10.15. Material Extended to the First Synchronization Point

As we progress, we should make notes in the "Contour Change Tracker." Methodical use of the "Contour Change Tracker" ensures there are effective musical changes at important synchronization points. In this case, we should note the arrival to the G major triad and the decrease in the rhythmic subdivision at 00:00:21:05. Figure 10.16 makes notes in the "Contour Change Tracker."

CONTOUR CHANGE TRACKER

Timing	0:00	21:05	25:18	31:22	32:04	35:15
Plot and Picture Event	Beginning	Mountains	VO Starts	VO Stops	Mountains	VO Starts
Instrumentation Increase						
Instrumentation Decrease						
Change Foreground Tone Color	Horns					
Change Scale Type						
Move Tonic						
Increase Dissonance Level						
Decrease Dissonance Level						
Increase Harmonic Rhythm						
Decrease Harmonic Rhythm						
Arrive at Significant Harmony	G5	G Triad				
Introduce a New Melody or Musical idea	X					
Restate a Previous Theme						
End a Melody or Musical Idea						
Change Melodic Phrasing						
Change Meter						
Change Rhythmic Emphasis within the Meter						
Increase Beat Subdivision						
Decrease Beat Subdivision		X				
Increase Tempo						
Decrease Tempo						
Start the Music	X					
Stop the Music						
Change Overall Composition Structure						
Change Overall Pitch Register						
Change Dynamic Markings	f					
Change Performance Techniques						
Change Recording Techniques						

FIG. 10.16. Contour Change Tracker up to the First Synchronization Point

Next, the narration begins at 00:00:25:18. To accommodate the narration, the music must shift to the background. In our case, we can reduce instrumentation by pulling out percussion and brass. We can also have the violins fade out, contracting the music to the low and mid registers. We can reduce the notated dynamic markings, shifting from forte to piano. In addition, we can have the horn melody fade out completely—and not replace it with another melody that may distract from the narration. Figure 10.17 makes these additions in our notated sketch. Figure 10.18 adds these changes to the "Contour Change Tracker."

Audio 17   Video 11v

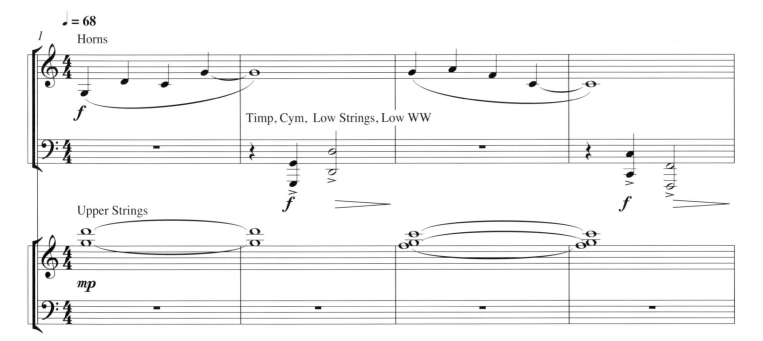

FIG. 10.17. Material Extended as the Narration Enters

CONTOUR CHANGE TRACKER

Timing	0:00	21:05	25:18	31:22	32:04	35:15
Plot and Picture Event	Beginning	Mountains	VO Starts	VO Stops	Mountains	VO Starts
Instrumentation Increase						
Instrumentation Decrease			X			
Change Foreground Tone Color	Horns					
Change Scale Type						
Move Tonic						
Increase Dissonance Level						
Decrease Dissonance Level						
Increase Harmonic Rhythm						
Decrease Harmonic Rhythm						
Arrive at Significant Harmony	G5	G Triad				
Introduce a New Melody or Musical idea	X					
Restate a Previous Theme						
End a Melody or Musical Idea						
Change Melodic Phrasing						
Change Meter						
Change Rhythmic Emphasis within the Meter						
Increase Beat Subdivision						
Decrease Beat Subdivision		X				
Increase Tempo						
Decrease Tempo						
Start the Music	X					
Stop the Music						
Change Overall Composition Structure			No Melody			
Change Overall Pitch Register			X			
Change Dynamic Markings	f		pp			
Change Performance Techniques						
Change Recording Techniques						

FIG. 10.18. Updated Contour Change Tracker

Next, the narration pauses at 00:00:31:22. This is immediately followed by a picture cut at 00:00:32:04. The narration then restarts at 00:00:35:15. This sequence of events is an opportunity for the music to expand—but only temporarily. To accomplish this, the melodic horns can reenter, playing a few notes reminiscent of the initial melodic idea. The chords can move more quickly than in previous measures, increasing harmonic rhythm. We can also increase rhythm in the melody, returning to the faster quarter notes. After the music expands for a few beats, we can reverse all of these effects, returning to sustained textures and removing the melody. Figure 10.19 makes these additions in the notated sketch. Figure 10.20 adds these changes to the "Contour Change Tracker."

Audio 18   Video 12v

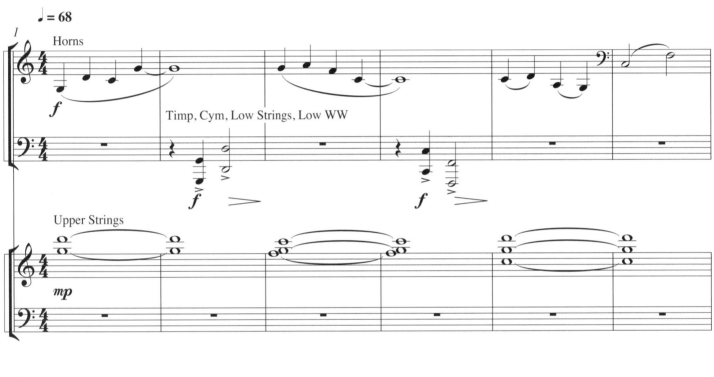

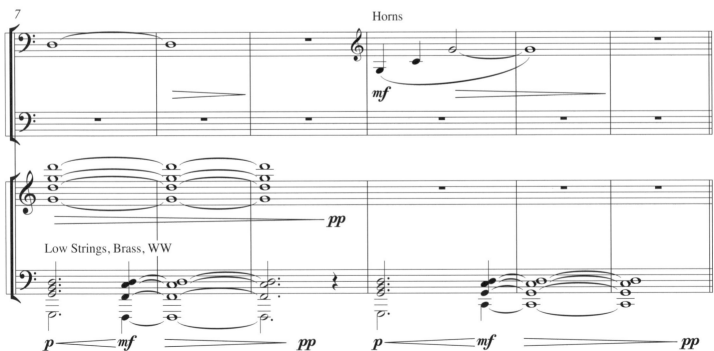

FIG. 10.19. Music Temporarily Expands During Pause in Narration

CONTOUR CHANGE TRACKER

Timing	0:00	21:05	25:18	31:22	32:04	35:15
Plot and Picture Event	Beginning	Mountains	VO Starts	VO Stops	Mountains	VO Starts
Instrumentation Increase					X	
Instrumentation Decrease			X			
Change Foreground Tone Color	Horns					
Change Scale Type						
Move Tonic						
Increase Dissonance Level						
Decrease Dissonance Level						
Increase Harmonic Rhythm					X	
Decrease Harmonic Rhythm						
Arrive at Significant Harmony	G5	G Triad				
Introduce a New Melody or Musical idea	X					
Restate a Previous Theme						
End a Melody or Musical Idea						
Change Melodic Phrasing						
Change Meter						
Change Rhythmic Emphasis within the Meter						
Increase Beat Subdivision					X	
Decrease Beat Subdivision		X				
Increase Tempo						
Decrease Tempo						
Start the Music	X					
Stop the Music						
Change Overall Composition Structure			No Melody		Melody	
Change Overall Pitch Register			X			
Change Dynamic Markings	f		pp		mf	
Change Performance Techniques						
Change Recording Techniques						

FIG. 10.20. Updated Contour Change Tracker

The previous visual idea—a pause in the narration paired with a picture cut—repeats itself between 00:00:43:24 and 00:00:45:12. Logically, it makes sense to reuse the same techniques. The melodic horn can temporarily reenter and the harmonic rhythm can pick up. After briefly expanding, the music can recede behind the reentering narration by arriving on sustained chords. Notably, the blowing snow visual occurs just prior to this at 00:00:39:26. Here, we can add a short melodic idea in violin, giving the music a new foreground tone color and faster rhythmic subdivision. Figure 10.21 extends the music through the next pause in the narration. Figure 10.22 updates the "Contour Change Tracker."

FIG. 10.21. Music Extended to Next Pause in Narration

CONTOUR CHANGE TRACKER

Timing	0:00	21:05	25:18	31:22	32:04	35:15
Plot and Picture Event	Beginning	Mountains	VO Starts	VO Stops	Mountains	VO Starts
Instrumentation Increase					X	
Instrumentation Decrease			X			X
Change Foreground Tone Color	Horns					
Change Scale Type						
Move Tonic						
Increase Dissonance Level						
Decrease Dissonance Level						
Increase Harmonic Rhythm					X	
Decrease Harmonic Rhythm						X
Arrive at Significant Harmony	G5	G Triad				
Introduce a New Melody or Musical idea	X					
Restate a Previous Theme						
End a Melody or Musical Idea						
Change Melodic Phrasing						
Change Meter						
Change Rhythmic Emphasis within the Meter						
Increase Beat Subdivision					X	
Decrease Beat Subdivision		X				X
Increase Tempo						
Decrease Tempo						
Start the Music	X					
Stop the Music						
Change Overall Composition Structure			No Melody		Melody	No Melody
Change Overall Pitch Register			X			
Change Dynamic Markings	f		pp		mf	p
Change Performance Techniques						
Change Recording Techniques						

CONTOUR CHANGE TRACKER

Timing	39:26	43:24	44:12	45:23	51:22	55:03
Plot and Picture Event	Blizzard	VO Stops	Mountains	VO Starts	Lone Hiker	VO Stops
Instrumentation Increase			X			
Instrumentation Decrease				X		
Change Foreground Tone Color	Violin		Horns			
Change Scale Type						
Move Tonic						
Increase Dissonance Level						
Decrease Dissonance Level						
Increase Harmonic Rhythm			X			
Decrease Harmonic Rhythm				X		
Arrive at Significant Harmony						
Introduce a New Melody or Musical idea						
Restate a Previous Theme						
End a Melody or Musical Idea						
Change Melodic Phrasing						
Change Meter						
Change Rhythmic Emphasis within the Meter						
Increase Beat Subdivision	X					
Decrease Beat Subdivision				X		
Increase Tempo						
Decrease Tempo						
Start the Music						
Stop the Music						
Change Overall Composition Structure	Melody					
Change Overall Pitch Register						
Change Dynamic Markings			mf	p		
Change Performance Techniques						
Change Recording Techniques						

FIG. 10.22. Updated Contour Change Tracker

Next, the visuals shift to the image of the isolated hiker at 00:00:51:22. At 00:00:55:03, the narration stops followed by the hiker's on-screen interview. The end of the narration acts as a conclusion to that section of the story. Musically, we can reinforce that by arriving on a cadence in the pause between the exiting narration and entering hiker dialogue. In this case, the pause between the narration and interview falls on beat 4 of the measure. We can move that to beat 1 by inserting a 3/4 measure into the phrase. To reinforce the isolation of the lone hiker, we can pull back to small instrumentation during the cadence, arriving on a single note rather than a full chord. Placing the single note in violins makes the moment even more tender. A cadence to a single note is also a change in pitch register, in this case entirely removing the low register. This single violin note can then fade out, exiting as we begin to see the image of the on-screen interview. Figure 10.23 extends the music to the on-screen interview, and figure 10.24 updates the "Contour Change Tracker."

FIG. 10.23. Music Extended to the On-Screen Interview

CONTOUR CHANGE TRACKER

Timing	0:00	21:05	25:18	31:22	32:04	35:15
Plot and Picture Event	Beginning	Mountains	VO Starts	VO Stops	Mountains	VO Starts
Instrumentation Increase					X	
Instrumentation Decrease			X			X
Change Foreground Tone Color	Horns					
Change Scale Type						
Move Tonic						
Increase Dissonance Level						
Decrease Dissonance Level						
Increase Harmonic Rhythm					X	
Decrease Harmonic Rhythm						X
Arrive at Significant Harmony	G5	G Triad				
Introduce a New Melody or Musical idea	X					
Restate a Previous Theme						
End a Melody or Musical Idea						
Change Melodic Phrasing						
Change Meter						
Change Rhythmic Emphasis within the Meter						
Increase Beat Subdivision					X	
Decrease Beat Subdivision		X				X
Increase Tempo						
Decrease Tempo						
Start the Music	X					
Stop the Music						
Change Overall Composition Structure			No Melody		Melody	No Melody
Change Overall Pitch Register			X			
Change Dynamic Markings	f		pp		mf	p
Change Performance Techniques						
Change Recording Techniques						

CONTOUR CHANGE TRACKER

Timing	39:26	43:24	44:12	45:23	51:22	55:03
Plot and Picture Event	Blizzard	VO Stops	Mountains	VO Starts	Lone Hiker	VO Stops
Instrumentation Increase			X			
Instrumentation Decrease				X	X	X
Change Foreground Tone Color	Violin		Horns		Violins	
Change Scale Type						
Move Tonic						
Increase Dissonance Level						
Decrease Dissonance Level						
Increase Harmonic Rhythm			X			
Decrease Harmonic Rhythm				X		
Arrive at Significant Harmony						G Unison
Introduce a New Melody or Musical idea						
Restate a Previous Theme						
End a Melody or Musical Idea						
Change Melodic Phrasing						
Change Meter						
Change Rhythmic Emphasis within the Meter						
Increase Beat Subdivision	X					
Decrease Beat Subdivision				X		
Increase Tempo						
Decrease Tempo						
Start the Music						
Stop the Music						
Change Overall Composition Structure	Melody					
Change Overall Pitch Register						X
Change Dynamic Markings			mf	p		pp
Change Performance Techniques						
Change Recording Techniques						

CONTOUR CHANGE TRACKER

Timing	56:29	59:28	1:03:00	1:12:27	1:15:18	1:25:24
Plot and Picture Event	Dlg. Starts	Headshot	Starry Sky	Dlg. Stops	VO Starts	End
Instrumentation Increase						
Instrumentation Decrease						
Change Foreground Tone Color						
Change Scale Type						
Move Tonic						
Increase Dissonance Level						
Decrease Dissonance Level						
Increase Harmonic Rhythm						
Decrease Harmonic Rhythm						
Arrive at Significant Harmony						
Introduce a New Melody or Musical idea						
Restate a Previous Theme						
End a Melody or Musical Idea		X				
Change Melodic Phrasing						
Change Meter						
Change Rhythmic Emphasis within the Meter						
Increase Beat Subdivision						
Decrease Beat Subdivision						
Increase Tempo						
Decrease Tempo						
Start the Music						
Stop the Music		X				
Change Overall Composition Structure						
Change Overall Pitch Register						
Change Dynamic Markings						
Change Performance Techniques						
Change Recording Techniques						

FIG. 10.24. Updated Contour Change Tracker

At 00:01:03:00, a picture cut reveals an image of the nighttime sky. In the story, this is a shift to a new idea—the beauty of the nighttime sky rather than the majesty of the mountains. To reinforce the shift in the plot, the music should introduce a new idea. We can introduce the sound of choir, which is commonly associated with nighttime sky visuals in film scoring. Notably, there is a pause in the dialogue from 00:01:12:27 to 00:01:15:18. The pause is an opportunity for a musical event, such as an arrival to an important harmony. Figure 10.25 includes one possible idea for the starry sky. The idea begins on G, making for a smooth transition from the previous cue. It arrives on A major, a new harmony we have not yet heard, in the pause in the dialogue.

Audio 21   Video 15v

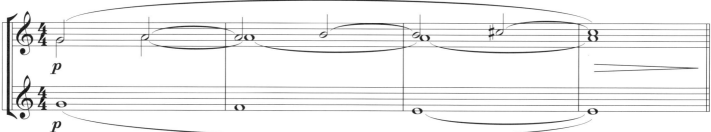

FIG. 10.25. Music for the Starry Sky

CONTOUR CHANGE TRACKER

Timing	0:00	21:05	25:18	31:22	32:04	35:15
Plot and Picture Event	Beginning	Mountains	VO Starts	VO Stops	Mountains	VO Starts
Instrumentation Increase					X	
Instrumentation Decrease			X			X
Change Foreground Tone Color	Horns					
Change Scale Type						
Move Tonic						
Increase Dissonance Level						
Decrease Dissonance Level						
Increase Harmonic Rhythm					X	
Decrease Harmonic Rhythm						X
Arrive at Significant Harmony	G5	G Triad				
Introduce a New Melody or Musical idea	X					
Restate a Previous Theme						
End a Melody or Musical Idea						
Change Melodic Phrasing						
Change Meter						
Change Rhythmic Emphasis within the Meter						
Increase Beat Subdivision					X	
Decrease Beat Subdivision		X				X
Increase Tempo						
Decrease Tempo						
Start the Music	X					
Stop the Music						
Change Overall Composition Structure			No Melody		Melody	No Melody
Change Overall Pitch Register			X			
Change Dynamic Markings	f		pp		mf	p
Change Performance Techniques						
Change Recording Techniques						

CONTOUR CHANGE TRACKER

Timing	39:26	43:24	44:12	45:23	51:22	55:03
Plot and Picture Event	Blizzard	VO Stops	Mountains	VO Starts	Lone Hiker	VO Stops
Instrumentation Increase			X			
Instrumentation Decrease				X	X	X
Change Foreground Tone Color	Violin		Horns		Violins	
Change Scale Type						
Move Tonic						
Increase Dissonance Level						
Decrease Dissonance Level						
Increase Harmonic Rhythm			X			
Decrease Harmonic Rhythm				X		
Arrive at Significant Harmony						G Unison
Introduce a New Melody or Musical idea						
Restate a Previous Theme						
End a Melody or Musical Idea						
Change Melodic Phrasing						
Change Meter						
Change Rhythmic Emphasis within the Meter						
Increase Beat Subdivision	X					
Decrease Beat Subdivision				X		
Increase Tempo						
Decrease Tempo						
Start the Music						
Stop the Music						
Change Overall Composition Structure	Melody					
Change Overall Pitch Register						X
Change Dynamic Markings			mf	p		pp
Change Performance Techniques						
Change Recording Techniques						

CONTOUR CHANGE TRACKER

Timing	56:29	59:28	1:03:00	1:12:27	1:15:18	1:25:24
Plot and Picture Event	Dlg. Starts	Headshot	Starry Sky	Dlg. Stops	VO Starts	End
Instrumentation Increase						
Instrumentation Decrease						
Change Foreground Tone Color			Choir, WW			
Change Scale Type						
Move Tonic						
Increase Dissonance Level						
Decrease Dissonance Level						
Increase Harmonic Rhythm						
Decrease Harmonic Rhythm						
Arrive at Significant Harmony			G	A		
Introduce a New Melody or Musical idea			X			
Restate a Previous Theme						
End a Melody or Musical Idea		X				
Change Melodic Phrasing						
Change Meter						
Change Rhythmic Emphasis within the Meter						
Increase Beat Subdivision						
Decrease Beat Subdivision						
Increase Tempo						
Decrease Tempo						
Start the Music			X			
Stop the Music		X				
Change Overall Composition Structure						
Change Overall Pitch Register						
Change Dynamic Markings						
Change Performance Techniques						
Change Recording Techniques						

FIG. 10.26. Updated Contour Change Tracker

The scene ends at 00:01:25:24 and the music should end accordingly. In this case, the conclusion has a sense of incompletion, leading the viewer to believe there is more to come. The music should likewise conclude with a sense of incompletion, propelling the viewer into the next scene. Previously, the harmony had arrived on a surprise A major triad. This is already a great start, as cadences to unexpected chords create a sense of incompletion. In addition, we can avoid ending the cue on a major triad. One option would be to have the strings enter on an open fifth A and E, and then have the low strings shift down to G and D. This creates the open and dramatic sound of stacked perfect fifths. Figure 10.27 adds this cadence to the cue, and figure 10.28 completes the "Contour Change Tracker."

Audio 22   Video 16v

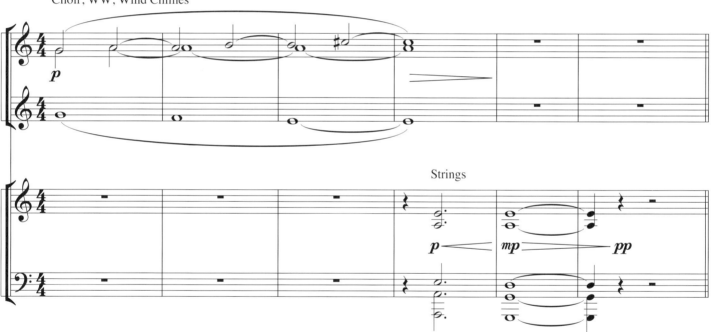

FIG. 10.27. Cadence for the End of the Scene

CONTOUR CHANGE TRACKER

Timing	0:00	21:05	25:18	31:22	32:04	35:15
Plot and Picture Event	Beginning	Mountains	VO Starts	VO Stops	Mountains	VO Starts
Instrumentation Increase					X	
Instrumentation Decrease			X			X
Change Foreground Tone Color	Horns					
Change Scale Type						
Move Tonic						
Increase Dissonance Level						
Decrease Dissonance Level						
Increase Harmonic Rhythm					X	
Decrease Harmonic Rhythm						X
Arrive at Significant Harmony	G5	G Triad				
Introduce a New Melody or Musical idea	X					
Restate a Previous Theme						
End a Melody or Musical Idea						
Change Melodic Phrasing						
Change Meter						
Change Rhythmic Emphasis within the Meter						
Increase Beat Subdivision					X	
Decrease Beat Subdivision		X				X
Increase Tempo						
Decrease Tempo						
Start the Music	X					
Stop the Music						
Change Overall Composition Structure			No Melody		Melody	No Melody
Change Overall Pitch Register			X			
Change Dynamic Markings	f		pp		mf	p
Change Performance Techniques						
Change Recording Techniques						

CONTOUR CHANGE TRACKER

Timing	39:26	43:24	44:12	45:23	51:22	55:03
Plot and Picture Event	Blizzard	VO Stops	Mountains	VO Starts	Lone Hiker	VO Stops
Instrumentation Increase			X			
Instrumentation Decrease				X	X	X
Change Foreground Tone Color	Violin		Horns		Violins	
Change Scale Type						
Move Tonic						
Increase Dissonance Level						
Decrease Dissonance Level						
Increase Harmonic Rhythm			X			
Decrease Harmonic Rhythm				X		
Arrive at Significant Harmony						G Unison
Introduce a New Melody or Musical idea						
Restate a Previous Theme						
End a Melody or Musical Idea						
Change Melodic Phrasing						
Change Meter						
Change Rhythmic Emphasis within the Meter						
Increase Beat Subdivision	X					
Decrease Beat Subdivision				X		
Increase Tempo						
Decrease Tempo						
Start the Music						
Stop the Music						
Change Overall Composition Structure	Melody					
Change Overall Pitch Register						X
Change Dynamic Markings			mf	P		PP
Change Performance Techniques						
Change Recording Techniques						

CONTOUR CHANGE TRACKER

Timing	56:29	59:28	1:03:00	1:12:27	1:15:18	1:25:24
Plot and Picture Event	Dlg. Starts	Headshot	Starry Sky	Dlg. Stops	VO Starts	End
Instrumentation Increase						
Instrumentation Decrease						
Change Foreground Tone Color			Choir, WW		Strings	
Change Scale Type						
Move Tonic						
Increase Dissonance Level						
Decrease Dissonance Level						
Increase Harmonic Rhythm						
Decrease Harmonic Rhythm						
Arrive at Significant Harmony			G	A	G5	
Introduce a New Melody or Musical idea			X			
Restate a Previous Theme						
End a Melody or Musical Idea		X				X
Change Melodic Phrasing						
Change Meter						
Change Rhythmic Emphasis within the Meter						
Increase Beat Subdivision						
Decrease Beat Subdivision						
Increase Tempo						
Decrease Tempo						
Start the Music			X			
Stop the Music		X				X
Change Overall Composition Structure						
Change Overall Pitch Register					X	
Change Dynamic Markings						
Change Performance Techniques						
Change Recording Techniques						

FIG. 10.28. Completed Contour Change Tracker

At this point, we can embellish any moments as we see fit. One possibility is to add some woodwind flourishes and percussion to the introduction. Such embellishments are common in large orchestrations in film scoring. In addition, they make the introduction even larger and more active, drawing contrast with the smaller instrumentation to come. The resulting full score is included in figure 10.29.

FIG. 10.29. Full Transposed Score for Scene from *Pacific Crest Trail*

The piece above is one possible score for this scene. However, it is not the one and only effective solution. As with any scene, there is more than one potential right answer. If a different composer were to score the scene based on our analysis, they would not write these same exact notes. However, their score could be equally effective to the final score presented here. In addition, a different creative team may push for a different answer to one of the framework questions, such as a different musical style. Changing the underlying analysis would lead to a different musical solution.

While there are always multiple possible right answers, there are also objectively ineffective musical ideas. Though we have focused primarily on using the framework to guide us to a viable musical score, it is equally effective at identifying ineffective scores.

Let's briefly consider an objectively ineffective score for this scene. The ineffective score is available in the media files (track 18v). Before noting what went wrong, let's observe there are some positive attributes to this cue. First, the cue is in the style of traditional orchestral film music, which is a defensible answer for musical style. Second, the cue does a wonderful job of accommodating dialogue, shifting to sustained textures and small instrumentation when the narration begins. Third, there are several contour moments that are quite effective, such as the low brass entrance on the picture cut to the mountains at 00:00:32:04.

Despite these positive attributes, the music goes awry in several ways. Most notably, the emotion of the music does not match the emotion of the scene. When we discussed emotion for the scene, we mentioned positive emotions—majesty, grandeur, beauty, and wonder. The music in the ineffective answer uses a low register melody based on minor thirds and tritones. This musical idea produces emotions that are dark, ominous, and sinister. Figure 10.30 shows the melody in the ineffective answer.

Audio 24   Video 18v

FIG. 10.30. Ineffective Melody for *Pacific Crest Trail*

In addition, the ineffective music has a higher energy level than the opening visuals. When we discussed energy level for the scene, we concluded the visuals had a low overall energy level. We gave it a 2 on a scale of 1 to 5. The ineffective answer begins with very large instrumentation, a tempo of 85 beats per minute, and an eighth-note subdivision. Musically, this produces a moderate to high energy level, likely a 3 or 4 on our scale of 1 to 5.

In the case of ineffective answers, the creative team can use the framework to conclude that the music is objectively wrong for a scene. In addition, the framework can pinpoint exactly what went wrong, be it an oversight in musical style, emotion, or other. Notably, a piece of music does not need to be wrong in every way to be ineffective. Rather, overlooking any single issue in the framework will lead to an ineffective solution. In addition, ineffective answers aren't necessarily bad music, they simply don't match a given scene. The ineffective answer presented here would be wonderful for an evil march, but it is wholly inappropriate for beautiful snowcapped mountains.

In film scoring, every scene has more than one possible right answer. Simultaneously, there are many objectively ineffective musical ideas for a scene. In this seemingly nebulous environment, the framework is a tool that provides a creative team with guidance. All potential effective answers share one characteristic—they are based on thoughtful and reasoned answers to the issues presented by the framework. Likewise, all ineffective musical solutions overlook at least one issue in the framework.

Worksheets

Blanks of these worksheets are available for download at www.halleonard.com/ mylibrary, using the unique code on the first page of this book.

A. STYLE DETERMINATION

Use this worksheet when deciding what musical style is most appropriate for the project. Each question focuses on an element of the project that may impact musical style, such as the geographical location of the plot. After answering questions 1 to 12, identify the desired musical style in question 13.

This worksheet is discussed in chapter 3.

STYLE DETERMINATION

1. What is the geographical location of the plot? Does the geographical location change during the film/scene? ___
___
___

2. What musical styles are associated with the geographical location(s)? ___
___
___

3. What is the time period location of the plot? Does the time period change during the film/scene? ___
___
___

4. What musical styles are associated with the time period(s)? ___
___
___

5. What musical styles are used in similar films and projects? ___
___
___

6. Should the music be similar to or different from these projects? ___
___

7. What studio or television network is the project for? ___
___

8. Is there a stylistic preference at that studio or television network? ___
___
___

9. What is the target demographic for the project? ___
___
___

Style Determination   1

10. What musical styles are appealing to the target demographic? _____
_____
_____

11. What musical styles are within the music budget for the project? _____
_____
_____

12. Are there any special considerations regarding musical style? _____
_____
_____

13. Desired musical style: _____
_____

B. STYLE CHARACTERISTICS

Use this worksheet when studying musical styles. Each question focuses on a characteristic of the music, such as overall instrumentation. After analyzing multiple pieces in a specific style, make note of any characteristics that recur in all pieces of that style. Also make note of any characteristics unique to the style, meaning they occur frequently in this style but rarely in other styles.

This worksheet is discussed in chapter 3.

STYLE CHARACTERISTICS

Style Name: _____

Instrumentation

Overall Instrumentation: _____

Melodic Instrumentation: _____

Harmony

Scale Type: _____

Chord Types: _____

Common Progressions: _____

Common Modulations (or lack thereof): _____

Harmonic Rhythm: _____

Melody

Common Melodic Intervals: _____

Melodic Phrasing: _____

Rhythm

Meter: _____

Beat Subdivision: _____

Tempo: _____

Common Rhythms: _____

Miscellaneous

Form: _____

Compositional Structure: _____

Performance Techniques: _____

Recording Techniques: _____

C. ANALYZING EMOTION

This worksheet includes a list of emotions commonly expressed in film. Peruse the list to identify an emotion that describes the emotional content of a scene. This worksheet is discussed in chapter 4.

ANALYZING EMOTION

Action	Contemplative	Expansive	Innocence	Patriotic	Soaring
Adrenaline	Contentment	Extreme	Intense	Peaceful	Sophisticated
Adventure	Coping	Fast	Intimate	Pensive	Sorrow
Aggression	Courage	Fear	Inspiring	Perseverance	Spiritual
Ambient	Creepy	Fearless	Instability	Persistent	Strength
Anticipation	Danger	Festive	Intense	Personal	Stress
Apprehension	Darkness	Finality	Introspective	Pity	Suspense
Anger	Denial	Floating	Investigative	Playful	Tender
Anxious	Despair	Flying	Ironic	Positive	Tension
Attack	Determined	Foreboding	Joy	Powerful	Terror
Awe	Disappointed	Forensic	Laid-back	Primal	Torment
Awkward	Disgust	Frantic	Laughter	Presidential	Traditional
Battle	Disoriented	Frenzied	Lighthearted	Progress	Tragedy
Beautiful	Distraught	Funny	Lonely	Prowling	Triumph
Big Finish	Disturbing	Futuristic	Love	Quiet	Trouble
Bittersweet	Doing Right	Getting Started	Lurking	Quirky	Uncertainty
Bold	Drama	Grief	Lush	Raw	Uneasy
Building	Dread	Gripping	Magical	Reflective	Unknown
Calm	Edge of Seat	Growing	Menacing	Relief	Unsettled
Carefree	Edgy	Guffaw	Motivated	Religious	Upsetting
Catastrophic	Eerie	Happy	Mysterious	Reminiscent	Urgency
Caution	Elegant	Heartbroken	Nail-biting	Resolution	Villain
Celebratory	Emotional	Heartwarming	Negative	Romance	Wistful
Celestial	Empathy	Helplessness	Nervous	Sad	Witty
Chase	Endearing	Hectic	Neutral	Satisfaction	Wonder
Childlike	Energetic	Heroic	Nobility	Scary	Worry
Clever	Escape	Hesitation	Nostalgic	Sentimental	Youth
Climactic	Ethereal	Historic	"Oh no!"	Serene	_____
Comedy	Euphoria	Honor	Old Fashioned	Serious	_____
Concern	Evil	Hope	On the move	Silly	_____
Conclusion	Evolving	Hopeless	Ominous	Sinister	_____
Conflict	Excitement	Horror	Pain	Sleepy	_____
Confusion	Expanding	Humorous	Panic	Sneaky	_____

D. STUDYING EMOTION IN MUSIC

Use this worksheet when studying emotion in music. Each question focuses on a characteristic of the music, such as overall instrumentation. After analyzing multiple pieces that produce a given emotion, make note of any characteristics that occur repeatedly.

This worksheet is discussed in chapter 4.

STUDYING EMOTION IN MUSIC

Emotion: _____

Instrumentation

Overall Instrumentation: _____

Melodic Instrumentation: _____

Harmony

Scale Type: _____

Chord Types: _____

Common Progressions: _____

Common Modulations: _____

Harmonic Rhythm: _____

Melody

Common Melodic Intervals: _____

Melodic Phrasing: _____

Rhythm

Meter: _____

Beat Subdivision: _____

Tempo: _____

Common Rhythms: _____

Miscellaneous

Form: _____

Compositional Structure: _____

Performance Techniques: _____

Recording Techniques: _____

E. VISUAL ENERGY ANALYSIS

Use this worksheet when analyzing the visual energy of a scene. Each question focuses on an element of the visuals that contributes to the energy level, such as movement of on-screen objects. After answering questions 1 to 5, identify the overall visual energy in question 6.

This worksheet is discussed in chapter 5.

VISUAL ENERGY ANALYSIS

1. How much movement is there in on-screen characters and objects?

1	2	3	4	5
very little		moderate		a great deal

2. How frequently do picture cuts occur?

1	2	3	4	5
rarely		occasionally		frequently

3. What type of picture cuts are used?

1	2	3	4	5
slow crossfades				hard cuts

4. Does the vantage point of the camera change via zooming or panning?

1	2	3	4	5
rarely		occasionally		frequently

5. Is the camera itself moving?

1	2	3	4	5
no		slowly		quickly

6. The overall visual energy level:

1	2	3	4	5
low		medium		high

F. ANALYZING MUSICAL ENERGY

Use this worksheet when analyzing the energy level of a piece of music. Each question focuses on an element of the music that contributes to the energy level, such as tempo. After answering questions 1 to 5, identify the overall musical energy in question 6.

This worksheet is discussed in chapter 5.

ANALYZING MUSICAL ENERGY

1. What is the tempo?

1	2	3	4	5
slow		moderate		fast
(60 bpm or less)				(160 bpm or more)

2. What is the rhythmic subdivision of the beat?

1	2	3	4	5
quarter note or less		eighth note		sixteenth note
(≤1 subdivision)		(2 subdivisions)		(≥4 subdivisions)

3. How large is the instrumentation?

1	2	3	4	5
small		medium		large

4. How frequently do the chords change (harmonic rhythm)?

1	2	3	4	5
rarely		occasionally (every measure)		frequently (every beat)

5. How frequently does the key change (modulations)?

1	2	3	4	5
never		occasionally		frequently (every couple of measures)

6. The overall musical energy is:

1	2	3	4	5
low		medium		high

G. DIALOGUE AND SOUND EFFECTS

Use this worksheet when analyzing the dialogue and sound effects of a scene. Questions 1 to 5 help determine if the music should be foreground or background material. If the music must be background material, then question 6 details compositional methods that help music recede to the background.

This worksheet is discussed in chapter 6.

DIALOGUE AND SOUND EFFECTS

1. Is there dialogue?   Yes   No

2. Is there anywhere the dialogue stops or pauses?   Yes   No

3. If there are breaks in the dialogue, where are they located? _____
_____
_____

4. Are there sound effects?   Yes   No
   If there are sound effects, are they foreground or background material? _____

5. Given the answers to questions 1 to 4, should the music be foreground or background material? _____
_____
_____

6. The following compositional techniques help music recede to the background. Which can be applied to the scene?

   ☐ No music at all

   ☐ Small instrumentation

   ☐ Soft tone colors

   ☐ Sustained textures

   ☐ Predictability in the musical structure

   ☐ Use a condensed pitch range

   ☐ No or minimized melody

   ☐ Avoid musical tone colors that are similar to the foreground tone color

H. CHARACTERISTICS OF CHANGE IN MUSIC

Use this worksheet when deciding what aspects of the music to change at a sync point. Each item on the list is a characteristic of the music that can change when there is a change in the picture. Most hits (changes in the music synchronized with changes in the picture) incorporate more than one element on the list.

This worksheet is discussed in chapter 7.

CHARACTERISTICS OF CHANGE IN MUSIC

Instrumentation

Increase/Decrease Overall Instrumentation: _____

Change Foreground Tone Color: _____

Harmony

Change Scale Type: _____

Move Tonic: _____

Increase/Decrease Dissonance Level: _____

Increase/Decrease Harmonic Rhythm: _____

Arrive at a Significant Harmony: _____

Melody

Introduce a New Melody or Musical Idea: _____

Restate a Previous Theme: _____

End a Melody or Musical Idea: _____

Change Melodic Phrasing: _____

Rhythm

Change Meter: _____

Change Rhythmic Emphasis within the Meter: _____

Increase/Decrease Beat Subdivision: _____

Increase/Decrease Tempo: _____

Miscellaneous

Stop/Start the Music: _____

Change Overall Compositional Structure: _____

Change Overall Pitch Register: _____

Change Dynamic Markings: _____

Change Performance Techniques: _____

Change Recording Techniques: _____

I. CONTOUR CHANGE TRACKER

Use this worksheet when tracking changes in contour. Timings and plot events specific to a scene can be detailed in the top two rows. After deciding what characteristics of the music to change at a given timing, mark the corresponding box with an X.

This worksheet is discussed in chapter 7.

CONTOUR CHANGE TRACKER

Timing					
Plot and Picture Event					
Instrumentation Increase					
Instrumentation Decrease					
Change Foreground Tone Color					
Change Scale Type					
Move Tonic					
Increase Dissonance Level					
Decrease Dissonance Level					
Increase Harmonic Rhythm					
Decrease Harmonic Rhythm					
Arrive at Significant Harmony					
Introduce a New Melody or Musical idea					
Restate a Previous Theme					
End a Melody or Musical Idea					
Change Melodic Phrasing					
Change Meter					
Change Rhythmic Emphasis within the Meter					
Increase Beat Subdivision					
Decrease Beat Subdivision					
Increase Tempo					
Decrease Tempo					
Start the Music					
Stop the Music					
Change Overall Composition Structure					
Change Overall Pitch Register					
Change Dynamic Markings					
Change Performance Techniques					
Change Recording Techniques					

J. ISSUES IN FORM

Use this worksheet when organizing the musical form for the project. Each question focuses on an element of the project that may impact musical form.

This worksheet is discussed in chapter 8.

ISSUES IN FORM

1. What are the literary themes of the film, and what emotions do we expect the audience to experience during the film?

_____

_____

_____

2. Is traditional leitmotif appropriate for this film? _____

_____

_____

_____

3. For each literary theme, is it most effective to attach a leitmotif, recurring motive, recurring emotional genre, or recurring musical style? _____

_____

_____

_____

4. What scenes should and should not have music? _____

_____

_____

_____

5. What scenes should have source music? _____

_____

_____

_____

6. What scene should have the biggest music? What scene should have the smallest music? _____

_____

_____

_____

7. When is the emotional climax of the film? _____

_____

_____

_____

INDEX

ABOUT THE AUTHOR

Ben Newhouse is a composer of film and concert music. Newhouse's commercial music has been used in over 3,000 episodes of television, including projects for ABC, CBS, NBC, and most major cable networks. Newhouse was awarded the BMI Pete Carpenter Fellowship in 1999.

Newhouse's orchestral music has been performed by the Texarkana Symphony Orchestra, the Eastman School Symphonic Orchestra, the William and Mary

Photo: Craig Reed

Symphony Orchestra, and the Pennsylvania Governor's School for the Arts Symphony Orchestra. Newhouse's overture *Heat* was awarded the "Howard Hanson Prize" for excellence in orchestral composition. Newhouse's *Fantasy for Strings* won the "Original Works Award" at the 2015 Orchestra Cup. Newhouse's chamber music has been performed by various groups around the United States, Europe, and Asia, including the Zodiac Trio from France and Talespin in Vienna.

Newhouse is a course author and instructor in the Continuing Education division of Berklee College of Music. He designed and oversees four courses in orchestration and film scoring. The University Continuing Education Association awarded his Orchestration 1 course "Best New Online Course" in 2009, and Berklee awarded Newhouse the "Distinguished Faculty Award" in 2015. Newhouse has also guest lectured at Pescara Conservatory in Pescara, Italy and Sydney Conservatorium of Music in Sydney, Australia.

Newhouse is a magna cum laude alumnus of the Eastman School of Music. He is a full-fellowship master's degree alumnus of the University of Southern California, completing a masters in business administration and a Business of Entertainment graduate certificate program with the School of Cinematic Arts.

More Fine Publications

Berklee Press

GUITAR

BEBOP GUITAR SOLOS
by Michael Kaplan
00121703 Book............................$16.99

BLUES GUITAR TECHNIQUE
by Michael Williams
50449623 Book/Online Audio...........$24.99

BERKLEE GUITAR CHORD DICTIONARY
by Rick Peckham
50449546 Jazz – Book.........................$12.99
50449596 Rock – Book.........................$12.99

BERKLEE GUITAR STYLE STUDIES
by Jim Kelly
00200377 Book/Online Media..........$24.99

CLASSICAL TECHNIQUE FOR THE MODERN GUITARIST
by Kim Perlak
00148781 Book/Online Audio.............$19.99

CONTEMPORARY JAZZ GUITAR SOLOS
by Michael Kaplan
00143596 ....$16.99

CREATIVE CHORDAL HARMONY FOR GUITAR
by Mick Goodrick and Tim Miller
50449613 Book/Online Audio.............$19.99

FUNK/R&B GUITAR
by Thaddeus Hogarth
50449569 Book/Online Audio...........$19.99

GUITAR CHOP SHOP – BUILDING ROCK/METAL TECHNIQUE
by Joe Stump
50449601 Book/Online Audio............$19.99

GUITAR SWEEP PICKING
by Joe Stump
00151223 Book/Online Audio.............$19.99

INTRODUCTION TO JAZZ GUITAR
by Jane Miller
00125041 Book/Online Audio $19.99

JAZZ GUITAR FRETBOARD NAVIGATION
by Mark White
00154107 Book/Online Audio $19.99

JAZZ SWING GUITAR
by Jon Wheatley
00139935 Book/Online Audio.............$19.99

A MODERN METHOD FOR GUITAR*
by William Leavitt
Volume 1: Beginner
00137387 Book/Online Video $24.99
*Other volumes, media options, and supporting songbooks available.

A MODERN METHOD FOR GUITAR SCALES
by Larry Baione
00199318 Book..........................$10.99

Berklee Press publications feature material developed at the Berklee College of Music.
To browse the complete Berklee Press Catalog, go to
www.berkleepress.com

BASS

BASS LINES
Fingerstyle Funk
by Joe Santerre
50449542 Book/Online Audio $19.95
Metal
by David Marvuglio
00122465 Book/Online Audio.............$19.99
Rock
by Joe Santerre
50449478 Book/CD $19.95

BERKLEE JAZZ BASS
by Rich Appleman, Whit Browne, and Bruce Gertz
50449636 Book/Online Audio $19.99

FUNK BASS FILLS
by Anthony Vitti
50449608 Book/Online Audio...........$19.99

INSTANT BASS
by Danny Morris
50449502 Book/CD $9.99

VOICE

BELTING
by Jeannie Gagné
00124984 Book/Online Media............$19.99

THE CONTEMPORARY SINGER – 2ND ED.
by Anne Peckham
50449595 Book/Online Audio $24.99

JAZZ VOCAL IMPROVISATION
by Mili Bermejo
00159290 Book/Online Audio $19.99

TIPS FOR SINGERS
by Carolyn Wilkins
50449557 Book/CD...............................$19.95

VOCAL TECHNIQUE
featuring Anne Peckham
50448038 DVD.....................................$19.95

VOCAL WORKOUTS FOR THE CONTEMPORARY SINGER
by Anne Peckham
50448044 Book/Online Audio..........$24.99

YOUR SINGING VOICE
by Jeannie Gagné
50449619 Book/Online Audio $29.99

WOODWINDS/BRASS

TRUMPET SOUND EFFECTS
by Craig Pederson & Ueli Dörig
00121626 Book/Online Audio..............$14.99

SAXOPHONE SOUND EFFECTS
by Ueli Dörig
50449628 Book/Online Audio $15.99

THE TECHNIQUE OF THE FLUTE: CHORD STUDIES, RHYTHM STUDIES
by Joseph Viola
00214012 Book..........................$19.99

PIANO/KEYBOARD

BERKLEE JAZZ KEYBOARD HARMONY
by Suzanna Sifter
00138874 Book/Online Audio............$24.99

BERKLEE JAZZ PIANO
by Ray Santisi
50448047 Book/Online Audio $19.99

BERKLEE JAZZ STANDARDS FOR SOLO PIANO
Arranged by Robert Christopherson, Hey Rim Jeon, Ross Ramsay, Tim Ray
00160482 Book/Online Audio............$19.99

CHORD-SCALE IMPROVISATION FOR KEYBOARD
by Ross Ramsay
50449597 Book/CD..............................$19.99

CONTEMPORARY PIANO TECHNIQUE
by Stephany Tiernan
50449545 Book/DVD $29.99

HAMMOND ORGAN COMPLETE
by Dave Limina
50449479 Book/CD $24.99

JAZZ PIANO COMPING
by Suzanne Davis
50449614 Book/Online Audio $19.99

LATIN JAZZ PIANO IMPROVISATION
by Rebecca Cline
50449649 Book/Online Audio..........$24.99

SOLO JAZZ PIANO – 2ND ED.
by Neil Olmstead
50449641 Book/Online Audio...........$39.99

DRUMS

BEGINNING DJEMBE
by Michael Markus & Joe Galeota
00148210 Book/Online Video $16.99

BERKLEE JAZZ DRUMS
by Casey Scheuerell
50449612 Book/Online Audio.............$19.99

DRUM SET WARM-UPS
by Rod Morgenstein
50449465 Book......................................$12.99

A MANUAL FOR THE MODERN DRUMMER
by Alan Dawson & Don DeMichael
50449560 Book......................................$14.99

MASTERING THE ART OF BRUSHES – 2ND EDITION
by Jon Hazilla
50449459 Book/Online Audio...........$19.99

PHRASING: ADVANCED RUDIMENTS FOR CREATIVE DRUMMING
by Russ Gold
00120209 Book/Online Media...........$19.99

WORLD JAZZ DRUMMING
by Mark Walker
50449568 Book/CD $22.99

STRINGS/ROOTS MUSIC

BERKLEE HARP
Chords, Styles, and Improvisation for Pedal and Lever Harp
by Felice Pomeranz
00144263 Book/Online Audio $19.99

BEYOND BLUEGRASS
Beyond Bluegrass Banjo
by Dave Hollander and Matt Glaser
50449610 Book/CD $19.99

Beyond Bluegrass Mandolin
by John McGann and Matt Glaser
50449609 Book/CD $19.99

Bluegrass Fiddle and Beyond
by Matt Glaser
50449602 Book/CD $19.99

EXPLORING CLASSICAL MANDOLIN
by August Watters
00125040 Book/Online Media.......... $19.99

THE IRISH CELLO BOOK
by Liz Davis Maxfield
50449652 Book/Online Audio......... $24.99

JAZZ UKULELE
by Abe Lagrimas, Jr.
00121624 Book/Online Audio............ $19.99

BERKLEE PRACTICE METHOD

GET YOUR BAND TOGETHER
With additional volumes for other instruments, plus a teacher's guide.
Bass
by Rich Appleman, John Repucci and the Berklee Faculty
50449427 Book/CD $16.99
Drum Set
by Ron Savage, Casey Scheuerell and the Berklee Faculty
50449429 Book/CD $14.95
Guitar
by Larry Baione and the Berklee Faculty
50449426 Book/CD $16.99
Keyboard
by Russell Hoffmann, Paul Schmeling and the Berklee Faculty
50449428 Book/Online Audio $14.99

WELLNESS

MANAGE YOUR STRESS AND PAIN THROUGH MUSIC
by Dr. Suzanne B. Hanser and Dr. Susan E. Mandel
50449592 Book/CD $29.99

MUSICIAN'S YOGA
by Mia Olson
50449587 Book $17.99

THE NEW MUSIC THERAPIST'S HANDBOOK – 3RD EDITION
by Dr. Suzanne B. Hanser
00279325 Book................................. $29.99

AUTOBIOGRAPHY

LEARNING TO LISTEN: THE JAZZ JOURNEY OF GARY BURTON
by Gary Burton
00117798 Book $27.99

HAL•LEONARD®

Prices subject to change without notice. Visit your local music dealer or bookstore, or go to **www.berkleepress.com**

MUSIC THEORY/EAR TRAINING/ IMPROVISATION

BEGINNING EAR TRAINING
by Gilson Schachnik
50449548 Book/Online Audio $16.99

THE BERKLEE BOOK OF JAZZ HARMONY
by Joe Mulholland & Tom Hojnacki
00113755 Book/Online Audio........... $27.50

BERKLEE MUSIC THEORY – 2ND ED.
by Paul Schmeling
Rhythm, Scales Intervals
50449615 Book/Online Audio $24.99
Harmony
50449616 Book/Online Audio $22.99

IMPROVISATION FOR CLASSICAL MUSICIANS
by Eugene Friesen with Wendy M. Friesen
50449637 Book/CD $24.99

REHARMONIZATION TECHNIQUES
by Randy Felts
50449496 Book........................... $29.99

MUSIC BUSINESS

ENGAGING THE CONCERT AUDIENCE
by David Wallace
00244532 Book/Online Media.......... $16.99

HOW TO GET A JOB IN THE MUSIC INDUSTRY – 3RD EDITION
by Keith Hatschek with Breanne Beseda
00130699 Book.................................... $27.99

MAKING MUSIC MAKE MONEY
by Eric Beall
50448009 Book $27.99

MUSIC LAW IN THE DIGITAL AGE – 2ND EDITION
by Allen Bargfrede
00148196 Book.................................... $19.99

MUSIC MARKETING
by Mike King
50449588 Book.................................... $24.99

PROJECT MANAGEMENT FOR MUSICIANS
by Jonathan Feist
50449659 Book.................................... $27.99

THE SELF-PROMOTING MUSICIAN – 3RD EDITION
by Peter Spellman
00119607 Book.................................... $24.99

MUSIC PRODUCTION & ENGINEERING

AUDIO MASTERING
by Jonathan Wyner
50449581 Book/CD............................ $29.99

AUDIO POST PRODUCTION
by Mark Cross
50449627 Book.................................... $19.99

THE SINGER-SONGWRITER'S GUIDE TO RECORDING IN THE HOME STUDIO
by Shane Adams
00148211 Book $16.99

UNDERSTANDING AUDIO – 2ND EDITION
by Daniel M. Thompson
00148197 Book.................................... $24.99

SONGWRITING, COMPOSING, ARRANGING

ARRANGING FOR HORNS
by Jerry Gates
00121625 Book/Online Audio............ $19.99

BEGINNING SONGWRITING
by Andrea Stolpe with Jan Stolpe
00138503 Book/Online Audio $19.99

BERKLEE CONTEMPORARY MUSIC NOTATION
by Jonathan Feist
00202547 Book.................................. $17.99

COMPLETE GUIDE TO FILM SCORING – 2ND ED.
by Richard Davis
50449607 .... $29.99

CONTEMPORARY COUNTERPOINT: THEORY & APPLICATION
by Beth Denisch
00147050 Book/Online Audio......... $22.99

THE CRAFT OF SONGWRITING
by Scarlet Keys
00159283 Book/Online Audio........... $19.99

JAZZ COMPOSITION
by Ted Pease
50448000 Book/Online Audio $39.99

MELODY IN SONGWRITING
by Jack Perricone
50449419 Book.................................. $24.99

MODERN JAZZ VOICINGS
by Ted Pease and Ken Pullig
50449485 Book/Online Audio $24.99

MUSIC COMPOSITION FOR FILM AND TELEVISION
by Lalo Schifrin
50449604 Book $34.99

MUSIC NOTATION
PREPARING SCORES AND PARTS
by Matthew Nicholl and Richard Grudzinski
50449540 Book.................................. $16.99

MUSIC NOTATION
THEORY AND TECHNIQUE FOR MUSIC NOTATION
by Mark McGrain
50449399 Book.................................. $24.95

POPULAR LYRIC WRITING
by Andrea Stolpe
50449553 Book.................................. $15.99

SONGWRITING: ESSENTIAL GUIDE
Lyric and Form Structure
by Pat Pattison
50481582 Book.................................. $16.99
Rhyming
by Pat Pattison
00124366 2nd Ed. Book $17.99

SONGWRITING IN PRACTICE
by Mark Simos
00244545 Book.................................. $16.99

SONGWRITING STRATEGIES
by Mark Simos
50449621 Book.................................. $24.99

THE SONGWRITER'S WORKSHOP
Harmony
by Jimmy Kachulis
50449519 Book/Online Audio $29.99
Melody
by Jimmy Kachulis
50449518 Book/Online Audio $24.99

Study Music *with* Berklee Online

Study Berklee's curriculum, with Berklee faculty members, in a collaborative online community. Transform your skill set and find your inspiration in all areas of music. Build lifelong relationships with like-minded students on your own time, from anywhere in the world.

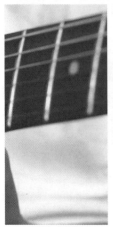